T0322744

BRIDGE OVER BLOOD RIVER

KAJSA NORMAN

Bridge Over Blood River

The Rise and Fall of the Afrikaners

HURST & COMPANY, LONDON

First published in Swedish in 2015 by Leopard förlag AB
as Bron över Blood River: Afrikanderna i det nya Sydafrika

First published in English in the United Kingdom in 2016 by
C. Hurst & Co. (Publishers) Ltd.,
41 Great Russell Street, London, WC1B 3PL
© Kajsa Norman, 2016
All rights reserved.

The right of Kajsa Norman to be identified as the author of
this publication is asserted by her in accordance with the
Copyright, Designs and Patents Act, 1988.

A Cataloguing-in-Publication data record for this book
is available from the British Library.

ISBN: 9781849046817

This book is printed using paper from registered sustainable
and managed sources.

www.hurstpublishers.com

The Publishers gratefully acknowledge permission to reproduce excerpts
from *My Traitor's Heart*, © 1990 by Rian Malan. Used by permission of
Grove/Atlantic, Inc. Any third party use of this material, outside of this
publication, is prohibited.

'We have triumphed in the effort to implant hope in the breasts of the millions of our people. We enter into a covenant that we shall build the society in which all South Africans, both black and white, will be able to walk tall, without any fear in their hearts, assured of their inalienable right to human dignity—a rainbow nation at peace with itself and the world. [...]

Never, never and never again shall it be that this beautiful land will again experience the oppression of one by another and suffer the indignity of being the skunk of the world.'

Nelson Mandela, inauguration as President of South Africa
10 May 1994, Pretoria

CONTENTS

CONTENTS

AUTHOR'S NOTE

South Africans live in a country 'where mutually annihilating truths coexist entirely amicably,' writes Rian Malan in his introduction to *Resident Alien*. His argument, in short, is that although the facts of any given story might be correct, one person's truth is always another person's lie.

I am certain that this coexistence of competing truths is the case in my story too. In South Africa, I'm not even a Resident Alien, but rather a complete alien, with no direct ties to the land. So, as an outsider, what makes my observations relevant?

I believe that all people are more or less blind to their own culture. Certainly, it has taken a decade away from my native Sweden for me to slowly begin to notice the peculiarities of my own culture; to realise that there are few things more Swedish than the naiveté displayed by our leading politicians when they claim there is no such thing as Swedish culture.

We are all products of our history, culture and context. They play a crucial role in determining our dreams and our fears. But sometimes it takes a perceived threat for a society to articulate its narrative and its values. And, frequently, it is not until we articulate something that we become fully aware of it.

By virtue of being an alien, of not being marked by South Africa's troubled and complex history, I hope I've been able to identify and give voice to some of the patterns and fears that characterise Afrikaner culture.

I lived in South Africa between 2011 and 2012 and it was during this time that most of my interviews and reportage took place. As such, certain facts or statistics may have changed, as well as the circumstances of some of the individuals portrayed in the book. Where relevant, I have updated the text to include more recent developments, but mostly the chapters provide snapshots of given moments and, as such, must remain unaltered.

It is also important to note that some of the names of individuals have been changed in order to protect their privacy. I'd like to thank all those who shared their stories and perspectives with me. Without their openness and honesty, this book could not have been written.

I'd also like to thank my husband Matthew for invaluable support and input, my editors and publishers in Sweden, the United Kingdom, and South Africa: Olav Fumarola Unsgaard, Moa Elf Karlén, Michael Dwyer, Jeremy Boraine, and Sophy Kohler, for believing in this book and helping to make it better. But most of all I'd like to express my gratitude to the late Henning Mankell who shepherded this story from start to finish. He kept me from giving up and insisted that this is an important story, relevant not only for South Africans, but for multicultural societies the world over.

I hope that you, the reader, will agree.

Kajsa Norman
London, July 2016

FOREWORD

THE EXPLORERS

Henning Mankell

In 1745, Professor Linné of Upsala University sent out his first student—or disciple, as he called them—on a botanical expedition to East India. The young man was called Ternström. The following year he would succumb to a tropical illness, adding his name to the list of the many young dead who Linné sent out, never to return. Another of Linné's disciples, perhaps the most talented of them all, Peter Forsskål from Swedish occupied Finland, travelled with a Danish expedition to the Arab countries. He didn't return home either. In the Yemeni city of Sana, he died, in terrible pain, from malaria. The sole legacy of his research, and his incessant botanical shipments to the impatiently awaiting Linné, was a nettle, which Linné named Forsskaolea.

Some of these disciples also traveled to Africa, which at the time was a well-mapped coastline circumscribing an empty black, or white, void beyond the coasts. Amongst these was Sparrman who provided significant insights about the still unidentified continent.

FOREWORD

Knowledge, on multiple levels, has always been brought home by travellers; brave, independent, and sometimes even rashly daring. 100 years after Linné and his disciples, the author Fredrika Bremer traveled America. She had a sharp eye and her travelogue about the vast country to the west was widely read. Breaking the gender barrier, Fredrika was the first Swedish woman to demonstrate an ability to observe and convey as great, if not greater, than the male explorers of her time.

From there it continued. New generations of travelers came and went. When I came of age in the early 1960s, there were many. The "report" was the hallmark of these authors and journalists. P. O. Enqvist mainly traveled around Sweden. Sara Lidman traveled everywhere, but focused on racist South Africa and Vietnam, as the small country fought, and eventually won its war against the USA. Sven Lindqvist made his greatest contributions exploring and writing in Latin America. Somewhere he wrote:

"Out of curiosity I opened the door in the wall".

I can't imagine a better image for the mission these explorers created for themselves.

Jan Myrdal and Gun Kessle traveled to Afghanistan, India and China. Anders Ehnmark sat in Rome for Expressen and wrote about the red Emilia, but he also had the entire African continent to cover, which of course was an impossible task.

But these explorers, some mentioned here, most of them not, kicked open the doors and windows of Sweden, creating a global cross-draft. We began to see ourselves in others. The world became as unjust and, in places, as terrible as we had probably suspected, but had been unable to prove. Now we could.

New explorers arise every day. During my many years in Africa, mainly Mozambique, I always tried to welcome young writers and give them the support we all need from time to time. The reward is often new texts and images, providing fresh perspectives on what the world is really like.

FOREWORD

One day a young lady from the north of Sweden comes to see me. Her name is Kajsa Norman. Thick-skinned and fearless, she has embarked on a daring journey through South Africa, deep into the landscapes of the tensions that still prevail there. It's soon clear to me that she represents the new generation. Her eye isn't mine, even though we both see what we see: Injustice, oppression of women, and the living, breathing racism that is not just a lingering ghost. We discuss her text. I learn that she belongs to the few who can actually take criticism and that she searches for the only thing worth seeking: that, which in the clearest and most unambiguous way, describes a society in a transition where there is every reason to be vigilant.

Kajsa Norman, it is then. Here are her observations from journeys in the country that not long ago kicked out the hateful system of apartheid and left it to die on the garbage pile of history.

PROLOGUE

15 December 2011. Banks of Blood River

An army of black clouds amasses on the distant hills. The air is tense as nature prepares for battle. I'm standing in an open field in KwaZulu-Natal, somewhere between the small towns of Dundee and Vryheid. Through these lands cut the muddy waters of Blood River.

I unpack my borrowed tent. The roof is ripped. The little aluminium pegs look like recycled coat hangers. During last night's blistering storm, thunder detonated around me like bombs. While I stayed in a solid wooden bungalow in the lush hills of Zululand, the wind rattled the windows and made the walls tremble. If tonight's storm is half as fierce, tomorrow they'll find pieces of my tent in Madagascar.

As I look around in bewilderment, a group of sturdy-looking men approach. They greet me in Afrikaans and proceed to ask me a series of questions I don't understand. I've been warned that English speakers aren't popular around these parts; that I should lie low and try to blend in. So much for that.

'Do you have family here?' the tallest one asks, in a thick accent.

'No. I'm a journalist. I'm writing about South Africa and was hoping I could sit in on the celebrations.'

PROLOGUE

They eye me suspiciously and talk among themselves.

'To learn more about Afrikaner culture,' I add tentatively.

Still no response.

'Are you English?' they ask.

'No,' I reply. 'Swedish.'

And that seems to help, because their eyes move from me to my cheap equipment, and they sigh with the realisation that I'm entirely at their mercy.

After conferring with one another for a few minutes they set off back to their camps. When they return, arms full of tools, the tension has dissipated. They get to work, disposing of my useless tent pegs and driving massive iron bars so far into the earth that I fear I'll never get them out again. Then they patch up the rip and tie my tent to a tree. I try to thank them, but they won't have it.

'It's not for you, it's for us. So we won't have to come rescue you from the middle of the river in the middle of the night. That's happened before, you know. Don't think your tent can't go flying just because you're in it.'

'Do you get a lot of storms?' I ask, steering the conversation away from my camping prowess.

'Almost every day at this time of year,' says the tall one, and he motions at their own camps securely tied down with thick ropes and iron hooks. It's clear a little bad weather isn't going to scare anyone off around these parts.

It is December 15, the day before the annual commemorations of the Battle of Blood River. Although celebrations are held at various locations across South Africa, many Afrikaner families have travelled from all over the country to this remote holy ground. Some spend as much as a week here, indulging in curious traditions. They play the 200-year-old Boerevolk sport of *jukskei*, where participants throw the wooden pins from oxen yokes at a stick planted in the ground. They gather mud in buckets from the river and compete to build the best clay oxen sculpture. They play traditional folk music on accordion and guitar. They pray. And they braai—a near spiritual version of the American barbeque.

When the men are finally done with my campsite, it would take a tornado to dislodge it. The big guy extends his hand and, for the first time, he smiles.

'Marius,' he says. 'Marius Verster. Welcome to Blood River.'

1

RISE OF THE SUBURBAN FORTRESS

'The barbarian tribes were arming, the rumor went; the Empire should take precautionary measures, for there would certainly be war.

Of this unrest I myself saw nothing. In private I observed that once in every generation, without fail, there is an episode of hysteria about the barbarians. There is no woman living along the frontier who has not dreamed of a dark barbarian hand coming from under the bed to grip her ankle, no man who has not frightened himself with visions of the barbarians carousing in his home, breaking the plates, setting fire to the curtains, raping his daughters. These dreams are the consequence of too much ease. Show me a barbarian army and I will believe.'

J.M. Coetzee, *Waiting for the Barbarians*

Everywhere I look, Johannesburg reminds me that it is one of the most dangerous cities in the world. Tall walls and electric fences have turned the homes of the middle class into fortresses. As I arrive from London in early October 2011, I can't decide which is more obtrusive, the oppressive heat or the omnipresent fear. I drive through the city, but see no houses, only walls.

I find a spot to rent in a tower in the affluent suburb of Sandton (at least when you're this high up, you don't need iron bars over your windows). When the sun isn't too intense, I sit on my balcony and look out over the sprawling township of Alexandra, one of South Africa's most notorious.

A few local white acquaintances warn me, incessantly, to adhere to a comprehensive set of safety rules: always lock the car doors; don't drive after dark, and if you absolutely must drive after dark, don't stop at 'robots'—the South African term for traffic lights; always know the exact route you're taking; don't venture into streets or neighbourhoods you aren't familiar with; be wary of vehicles or obstacles blocking a road; don't use public transport.

Some rules are more paranoid in their tone: don't trust the police (they will screw you), never walk anywhere (you will get mugged), don't talk to strangers (they will shoot you). And when taken together, they offer a distinct and rather alarming message: don't leave your fort (you will die).

As I find the idea of driving in Joburg almost more terrifying than the thought of being stabbed on a bus, ultimately I ignore the warnings. With a knot in my stomach I wave down one of the overcrowded minibuses that I have been warned against. While I am the only white person on the bus, I am neither attacked nor molested or robbed. Instead, the driver is friendly, carefully explaining to me how to find my destination and where to catch the bus back. When I take out my wallet to pay the five rand bus fare, he refuses my money. 'First ride is free!' he exclaims with a big smile, and takes off with squealing tyres.

To access my new home I have to scan my fingerprint three times: once to enter the lift, a second time to access my floor of the building, and a third time to enter my apartment. Then I enter a code to open the door. Security cameras allow the whole process to be supervised by armed guards. It takes a while to get used to the fact that the switch beside my bed doesn't control the lights: it's a panic button meant to trigger immediate armed response.

* * *

RISE OF THE SUBURBAN FORTRESS

My first Friday night in town I go for dinner with Mark, an entrepreneur. Like many white South Africans, he lives in a gated community, sheltered behind walls and barbed wire, with armed guards at the entrance. Still, break-ins do occur.

'I didn't know I was a racist growing up,' he tells me. 'It may seem stupid, but that's the way it was. I always knew I would have money. I always knew I'd drive a car like this one.' He gently strokes his BMW convertible.

I study Mark's face closely, scrutinising his features for signs of maliciousness, of inborn violence, but I find none.

Mark used to kill black people. And he is far from the only one. During apartheid all white South African men were legally obliged to perform military service, starting at sixteen, or alternatively the year after high school. Service lasted for two years. Between 1967 and 1994, approximately 600,000 young men were conscripted. Failure to sign up meant harsh penalties. The alternatives were to object on conscientious grounds (and face the possibility of a six-year jail sentence) or to flee the country. Thus, whether grudgingly or willingly, most white men now between the ages of around forty and sixty once served in the Army, Navy or Air Force. National service became widely regarded as a rite of passage from boyhood to manhood.

However, as the number of casualties grew, conscription turned into a hot political topic. How many men were killed while on active duty in defence of the Republic of South Africa remains unclear, but it is thought to be at least 2,000. After 1961, South African conscripts were sent straight from training to fully-fledged war zones, fighting battles in Angola in an effort to protect citizens from the *rooi gevaar* and the *swart gevaar*—the combined threats of communism and African nationalism. And when the domestic situation deteriorated, and rioting erupted in South Africa's townships, conscripts were sent to reinforce the police in what the government asserted was an effort to prevent civil war. In reality, these missions often supported the abuses of an aggressive and twisted police force. Mark once told me some even regarded trips to the townships as game drives, the residents as fair prey.

Many adult white South African men have killed, I repeat in my head, considering the words. Mark has killed for sure; I know that much. And not at some clinical, cold distance with a rifle from far away, but up close and personal, using a knife to slit the throats of enemies. He has made it clear he doesn't like to talk about this period of his life. Like most, he has worked hard to bury years of painful memories.

Uniting the military was an obvious first step in the process of reconciliation. Integrating the different armies into one would prove a challenging mission. Suddenly, people who had been fighting each other were meant to fight side by side, with the trust and respect of one aligned force. Under the circumstances most dealt with the situation pretty well, blaming politicians and understanding that fellow soldiers were just following orders and that now those orders had changed. For military commanders, however, integration was far tougher. After all, they were the ones who had issued the orders, and although they too had operated within a certain political context, their actions were harder to justify, not least to themselves. Many remained in denial until the very end, refusing to adapt. Some adapted eventually, faced with the threat of losing their jobs. Others left and became mercenaries in other African wars. Convincing black South Africans to forgive white South Africans turned out to be easier than expected. Persuading the white population to forgive themselves was, and continues to be, much more difficult.

As the election of 1994 approached, many Afrikaners who opposed the end of apartheid stocked up on food and hid in bunkers hoping to avoid extermination. Knowing they would lose power, they grabbed their guns and their Bibles, and prepared for war. But nothing happened. Days passed, then weeks, and still there was no attack. The media managed to capture some dazed, bearded men coming out of hiding, dirty and confused.[1] They had waited for the barbarians to come, but saw only their own haggard reflections staring back at them from TV screens across the nation. As journalist Rian Malan writes:

> Our ancestors bestrode Africa like giants, slaughtering game, digging holes for gold, subjugating everyone. When the tide turned, we steeled ourselves for Armageddon, but nothing happened. The enemy came to power, but no vengeance was taken. They were even willing to forgive us, provided that we fell to our knees and said sorry. I experienced this as totally humiliating. White males had become ridiculous, and we were heading towards irrelevance.[2]

As a result, Afrikaners were left with two options: to admit their mistakes, apologise and hang their heads in shame, or to deny any honourable intentions of those they had oppressed. Many opted for the latter, unable simply to discard an entire belief system overnight. Some were content with waiting behind high fences, interpreting any turn of events in the most negative light. Others went on to invent threats, manufacture fear, and consciously or unconsciously feed the nightmare of the barbarian lurking in the bush beneath the bedroom window.

* * *

South Africa's legacy of violence is likely one of the key drivers behind the country's frightening crime statistics. Since the turn of the century an average of close to 20,000 murders[3] and some several hundred thousand rapes are committed each year. When numbers like these are repeated often enough, and images of the victims are sprawled daily across the media, one quickly develops the habit of feeling grateful each evening for having made it through yet another day unharmed.

And the statistics don't even necessarily reflect the true scale of the crisis. According to former Deputy Justice Minister

Johnny de Lange, forensic investigations are only conducted on roughly half of all crime scenes and the police and legal institutions are only able to investigate a fraction of all the crimes committed.[4] There are not enough resources to cope with the caseload. As a result, when it comes to protecting the public, confidence in the police is all but gone. Between April 2011 and April 2012, 600 police officers were arrested for corruption in Gauteng province alone.

Most South Africans have therefore come to accept that security is something you buy; and that the more you pay, the safer you'll be. Private security agencies patrol most neighbourhoods. Buying protection from an armed response company is even mandatory to qualify for some home insurance plans. Still, many consider this insufficient and neighbours frequently join forces to create their own neighbourhood watch teams, carrying out additional patrols of their own. One of Mark's friends even organises hostage-freeing courses, where participants are taught to use explosives to 'quickly and safely' rescue loved ones held captive in their own homes. Few have faith that the police will arrive in time or be properly equipped to actually do anything meaningful in such situations.

Back in his car, Mark shows me the array of knives he carries. He drives with armoured gloves and has a stiletto knife in his pocket right next to his wallet. If anyone attempts to carjack him, he says he will simply pull it out to 'punch but miss' so that the blade of the stiletto will open up the stomach of the perpetrator.

'Then his guts will fall out in a bloody mess and his mates will rush to help him, leaving me free to escape,' explains Mark, who is convinced that no local travels without a weapon in Joburg.

As we're driving home, Mark slams on the brakes suddenly as a group of black youths unexpectedly step into the road.

'I'm done killing kids,' he says.

16 DECEMBER 1838

THE BATTLE OF BLOOD RIVER

'My brothers and fellow countrymen, we stand here now for a moment before a holy God of heaven and earth, to make a vow to Him. If He would give us his protection and be with us, and deliver our enemy into our hands so that we may defeat him, we shall pass this day and date each year as an anniversary, and honour it like a Sabbath, and we shall build a temple to His honour wherever it shall please Him, and we shall tell this to our children so that they may share in it with us, in remembrance also for our future generations, so that the glory of His name may be sanctified thereby, and the glory and honour of victory shall be given unto Him.'

The Vow, engraved at the Blood River Monument

The words of preacher Sarel Cilliers inspire courage and hope among the Boer families. A group of 464 men, women and children head east across southern Africa in search of a new home.

7

Every day during the past week they have repeated their vow to God, bargained with their Lord for a pact that will let them survive. The Zulu army is close now. It's time to prepare for battle.

By the Ncome River, the leader of the Boer families, Andries Pretorius, finds suitable terrain on which to build an improvised fort: a laager consisting of sixty-four wagons, carefully tied together in the shape of a half moon.

Shielded by darkness, the enemy approaches. When the morning mist lifts, thousands of mighty Zulu warriors materialise, not more than 40 m from the wagons. Row upon row of muscular bodies poise behind their cowhide shields.

Pretorius orders his men to open fire. Through the smoke he sees the sea of Zulu men rise as one. With raised spears and shrill screams, they charge. But the gunfire of the Boers cuts them short.

After two hours and four waves of attack, the Zulu retreat in chaos. Boer horsemen pursue the fleeing warriors. So many Zulu men are killed on the banks of the river that their blood turns the water red, earning the river its Afrikaans name: Bloedrivier.

When the battle is over, more than 3,000 Zulu warriors lie dead across the battlefield. The trekkers have not lost a single man.

* * *

In 1652, traders of the Dutch East India Company established a support station near what is today known as Cape Town.

Before the opening of the Suez Canal, virtually every ship travelling between Europe and Asia stopped there to stock up on supplies. This meant a high demand for fresh provisions and wine. At first, the local Khoikhoi herdsmen, whom the settlers referred to as Hottentots, in a derogatory imitation of the sound of the Khoikhoi language, traded supplies with the passing ships. However, recognising the opportunity, settlers soon began farming themselves, and ultimately displaced the Khoikhoi.

The colony grew into a settler community made up of former Company employees, lower-working-class Dutch, and Calvinist Protestants from France fleeing religious persecution. As the colony expanded, clashes between the settlers and the indigenous population became more frequent. The Khoikhoi who weren't killed through conflict or European diseases, were exploited as a source of cheap labour by wealthy settlers, who also imported slaves from Indonesia, India, Madagascar and Eastern Africa. Between 1652 and 1808, when the slave trade officially ended, approximately 63,000 slaves had been imported.[1]

Colonists pseudo-integrated the slaves into their families, first naming them, then governing them via a complex, 'extended family' type construct, later referred to as paternalism. This defined their social rights, obligations and, eventually, their transfer to other masters. Transfers were typically made to relatives, as the custom of the time was to keep the slaves in the family.[2]

Although some of the settlers undoubtedly became wealthy, far from all prospered. White domestic servants and dock labourers were not uncommon. However, these lower-class white workers were never bought and sold as slaves. Nor were they 'property', and although white workers suffered poor wages and frequent mistreatment, they were free to choose their manner of employment.[3]

Over time, Company officials began abusing their positions to obtain the best land and licences for wine, meat, fish and wheat. Corruption and nepotism grew. Unable and unwilling to live under such conditions, in 1710 many of the less influential settlers began to move into the interior, creating new districts. They became known as the Trekboers, and eventually, as Boers: nomadic livestock farmers roaming the frontier and beyond in search of pasture for their cattle. They lived in complete isolation from the rest of the world, untouched by the intellectual developments that dominated Europe in the eighteenth century.

Maps of the time showed the interior of Africa as almost entirely blank. Westerners considered it a place of darkness, populated by the most terrible creatures one could imagine: savage beasts and savage men. Out on the veld only the toughest survived. While most settlers were deterred by the brutality of the frontier, for some it created an almost perverse allure. Those who venture into the heart of darkness, as Joseph Conrad wrote, 'live in the midst of the incomprehensible, which is also detestable. And it has a fascination, too, that goes to work upon him.'[4]

Many who dared set out into these inhospitable lands eventually succumbed to the wilderness of their surroundings, or the wilderness of their own hearts. According to the author and journalist Rian Malan, who grew up in a conservative Afrikaans family in the 1960s, these ancestors of his 'lived by the gun, and according to the Old Testament. Its tales of tribes wandering the desert spoke to them.'[5] All that time spent in isolation on the frontier had transformed them into a people the British regarded as white barbarians—ignorant, unkempt and violent. In the words of Malan:

> They had become Afrikaners, the white tribe of Africa, arrogant, xenophobic, and 'full of blood,' as the Zulus say of tyrants. They had their own language, their own customs and traditions, and a myth to light their way, a mystic Christian mission on the Dark Continent. They spoke of themselves as bearers of the light, but in truth they were dark of heart, and they knew it, and willed it so. [...]

> On the frontier, it was an eye for an eye, and then an arm for an arm, and a leg for a leg, or so the Boers believed, and who is to say they were wrong? There was nothing in the Xhosa's history of expansion and conquest to suggest that they were any more willing to love than the white man. *Bloed roep om wraak. Siyabiza igazi wetho.* That was a saying on both sides of the frontier. It means, 'Spilled blood calls for vengeance.' In such a place, or so the Boers believed, a weak and doubtful man would soon be a dead one.

And so, when rumours of the Enlightenment penetrated their wilderness, the Afrikaners considered them, consulted their Bibles and preachers, and finally reached a consensus: These new ideas presented a threat to their survival, and should be suppressed—not only in the world at large, but in their own hearts. Soon, many Afrikaners were calling themselves Doppers, after the little metal caps with which they snuffed out candles. They called themselves Doppers because they were deliberately and consciously extinguishing the light of the Enlightenment, so that they could do what they had to do in darkness.[6]

As the Boers continued to push out from the colony, conflict with the indigenous Khoikhoi, San and Xhosa peoples increased. In 1795, when the regional Company governor refused to send a commando force after a Xhosa cattle raiding party, rebellion broke out. The governor was forced to leave, and the frontier Boers declared the region an independent district, refusing to pay Company taxes or obey their laws.

In an effort to bring the rebellion to submission, the colony cut off access to ammunition, making survival in such hostile territory increasingly difficult. Later that year, as the Dutch East India Company began to collapse under a mountain of debt, the British seized the opportunity and invaded the highly strategic Cape, placing the entire colony under British rule. At that point the colony consisted of approximately 25,000 slaves, 20,000 white colonists, 15,000 Khoisan and 350 freed black slaves. While the British quickly took control of politics, finance and trade, the rebellious spirit of the Afrikaners proved harder to subjugate.

Everyone was now a British subject and, as such, deemed to be equal before the law. However, for the first two decades of British occupation, not only did the Dutch colonists reject any form of status levelling, the laws themselves were not well suited to support the cultural differences of the Khoikhoi.

Since most Khoikhoi were not Christians, and thus unable to swear an oath, their evidence was given less credence in legal disputes with the white Christian population. Furthermore, while according to British law the indigenous people had the right to own land, their meagre incomes and assets made acquiring land a near impossibility.

Economics also conspired against British willingness to end slavery. Slaves represented about a sixth of the total value of a farm in the Cape Colony so any attack on slavery was also an attack on the farming community. But the economic roots of the evil extended well beyond farmers as slaves were the principal mortgageable assets in the colony. In spite of this deep entrenchment, public pressure in Britain to abolish the slave trade had built up to such an extent that the new British government at the Cape felt compelled to investigate the impact of ending the importation of slaves into the colony. In 1797, Willem Stephanus van Ryneveld, a progressive thinker, was tasked with examining whether the colony would survive if the import of new slaves were to be banned.

Van Ryneveld acknowledged that slavery had made the Boers 'lazy, haughty and brutal', but maintained that it had become 'a necessary evil', which could not be eradicated without sacrificing 'the Colony and perhaps the poor slaves that are in it'. Ending slavery, he predicted, would be the work 'not of years, but as it were of centuries'.[7]

* * *

In the early 1830s, the Eastern Cape suffered a severe drought, and grazing was soon exhausted. Meanwhile, the population grew, putting further pressure on demand for land and adding to the general sense of hardship and poverty.

In 1834, slavery was finally abolished. Although the Boers were allowed to keep their slaves as 'apprentices' for an additional four years, many felt they didn't receive enough compensation for the financial losses incurred when they had to set the slaves free.

The British also made it more difficult for Afrikaners to acquire land and put little effort into upholding law and order on the frontier. The frontiersmen lacked any formal protection and, as a consequence, were often raided by local tribes. They found themselves resenting the fact that their only contact with the government was the tax collector. Then the British set English as the only official language. Feeling increasingly marginalised and in constant conflict with the colony, the Afrikaners decided it was time to move on, and so began the Great Trek.[8]

'Voortrekker', the Afrikaans and Dutch word for pioneer, refers to someone who takes the lead, who treks ahead. During The Great Trek some ten thousand Afrikaners, not counting their many Coloured and black servants, set out to found their own state, independent of British rule. Here, the white man would be free to rule as he saw fit, while the black man would be kept subordinate.

The journey into the interior was not easy. Indigenous populations occupied much of the land they traversed, making armed conflict almost inevitable. Several groups of the original Voortrekkers were wiped out by a combination of fever and the hostility they encountered along their route.

In the 1830s most of the fertile lands of Natal, the Orange Free State and the Transvaal lay depopulated after the rampages of the Zulu king Shaka and Mzilikazi, king of the Ndebele. Shaka Zulu, sometimes referred to as Africa's Napoleon, had caused the extermination of some three million people. By the time the trekkers arrived in Natal, Shaka had been murdered and replaced by his half-brother, Dingaan. Voortrekker leader Piet Retief met with Dingaan and convinced him to allow the Boers to settle in the lands to the south of the Tugela and Mzinyathi rivers.

A thousand wagons soon gathered in Natal on the Bushman's River near the present town of Estcourt. The trekkers made themselves at home while trekker leader Piet Retief and a party of about a hundred men, including servants, set off to King Dingaan's settlement to formalise the land agreement and hand over some cattle. Dingaan promptly signed the treaty and the trekkers were then treated to great festivities and displays of Zulu dance. The Boers, for their part, offered shows of horsemanship and gunfire, racing their horses and firing their weapons in make-believe battles around King Dingaan's great arena. On the fourth day, as the trekkers were getting ready to leave, Dingaan convinced them to stay for a final farewell. They were asked to leave their weapons outside so as not to offend the king. Retief and his men complied. They were offered milk and beer while singing Zulu warriors surrounded them. The singing grew louder and louder. Then the dancing started. The king himself joined in as thousands of feet thundered in the dusty ground building up towards a climax. Then, suddenly, Dingaan signaled his men to halt and into the great silence that followed, he roared: 'Kill the wizards!' The warriors leapt forward, seized the Boers, dragged them out of the arena and up a hill where their skulls were smashed and their bodies left for the vultures.[9]

The reason for the killings remains unknown. Some say that the show the trekkers put on in the arena with their horses and muskets frightened Dingaan. If a mere hundred men could cause such a stir, larger numbers of them would pose a real threat to the Zulu nation. Others blame superstitions, arguing that the Zulu people believed the trekkers to be sorcerers. Some Afrikaners even claim that the British instigated the massacre by telling Dingaan that the Boers were deserters from their own king who had come to take Dingaan's land from him, and that the terror they displayed in the arena would soon be unleashed against Dingaan himself.

Once Piet Retief and his men were dead, King Dingaan dispatched his army to hunt down and exterminate the main trekker party. The Zulu warriors ran all day and most of the night. It was still dark when they caught up with the Boers who were not expecting the attack. It was an orgy of mutilation and disembowelment. Nobody was spared. The breasts of women and the genitals of men were hacked off and pushed into the mouths of the victims. Young children had their brains bashed out against wagon wheels. On 17 February 1838, some five hundred people were murdered at a site that Afrikaners would henceforth call Weenen, meaning 'to weep'.

While some contemplated retreat, others, especially the women, were overcome by a desire for vengeance and refused to leave the land that was now soaked with the blood of their children. The first attempts at revenge were unsuccessful, but in spite of suffering heavy losses, the Boers found ways to turn their defeats into heroic myths.

For example, on 6 April 1838, under the lead of Piet Uys and Hendrik Potgieter, a few hundred trekkers headed towards the Zulu kingdom on horseback. They rode straight into enemy territory knowing they'd be outnumbered by about a hundred to one. By the time they arrived, Dingaan was well aware that they were coming, and the element of surprise they were relying on had been eliminated. Dingaan easily trapped them in a valley at the foot of Itala Mountain and, while most Boers managed to escape on their horses, Piet Uys and eight of his men were cut off. Instead of fleeing when he had the chance, legend has it that Uys's twelve-year-old son Dirkie chose to stay behind and fight to the death alongside his wounded father. At the Voortrekker monument, large sections are dedicated to the story of Dirkie, who, through the tales of his bravery, secured a place for himself in the Afrikaner pantheon.

The Bible was the only book many of the trekkers ever read. The Old Testament influenced them greatly, and in the history of Israel they found a parallel to their own existence. In the eyes of the Boers, their crushing victory and accompanying absence of casualties on 16 December had more to do with the will of God than with their rifles and canons. They were a chosen people.

2

JC

With straight backs and pale faces, a row of blond children sit in front of a TV at the Blood River Museum. Peeking through their fingers, they watch as Piet Retief and his men are taken by the Zulu King Dingaan and brutally slaughtered in a dramatic historical reenactment. Then follows the story of the Battle of Blood River, of the great revenge, when the Lord helped the Boers defeat the barbarians.

The children emerge from the dark of the museum's screening room. They stand still for a moment, their eyes squinting as they readjust to the bright sunshine outside. Then they start running, a few tentative steps at first, then faster and more animatedly. It's time to play. Not Cops and Robbers, not Cowboys and Indians, but Zulu and Boer.

The museum shop is a clean, but rustic country affair displaying a diverse selection of souvenirs commemorating the battle. There are little tin cups and plates with BLOOD RIVER inscribed on them, horsewhips, the flags of the old Boer republics, trinkets and a small selection of books. On a wall in the far corner are two small shelves. On one sit a dozen or so DVDs about the Battle of Blood River, the Boer war, and what are described as 'other colonial adventures'. The other houses a collection of films on Adolf Hitler and the rise of the Third Reich.

Outside the shop, a chubby boy with a pinkish complexion, and blond hair tucked away in a baseball cap, stands smoking a cigarette. He looks like he is about twelve years old.

'Do your parents know you smoke?' I ask.

'Yes.'

'It's better he does it around the house than sneaks off somewhere,' says a voice behind me.

I turn around and face a middle-aged man with a neatly trimmed beard. He is the shopkeeper and the boy is his son, JC, who is eighteen and not twelve.

'There's nothing you can do to stop kids these days,' he says.

When I first arrived, I had watched JC mock wrestle with an older black man in the shop of the little museum. They were laughing and seemed to be friendly, so now I think to ask JC if he knows how the black workers feel about the Blood River commemoration. It is, after all, as much an act of veneration as it is a symbol of remembrance.

'They are intimidated. They stay away,' he replies.

'Do they complain about it?'

'No, if they did I would ...' He grows silent and raises his fist to deliver a punch through the air.

We start to walk across the grass towards the camp.

'Then how do you know they are intimidated?' I press.

'They think it's strange we're still celebrating this day, so they stay away.'

'Do you have any black friends?'

He shakes his head.

'But I saw you playing with a black man in there.'

'Oh, but he is apartheid.'

'What do you mean?'

'He still calls me boss. I told him he doesn't have to anymore, but he says he can't call me anything else.'

We walk in silence now. When the conversation resumes it quickly turns to crime, as I find small talk often does in this country. JC embarks on an extended lamentation on the atrocious levels of crime in South Africa.

'But there is crime everywhere,' I object.

'Yes, but here it's worse; it's racism. They're cowards, they attack in groups. And you know us Boers, we're not so good at staying down. We keep getting up until they get tired and in the end that's how we win.'

We arrive at my campsite and watch as a horse is unloaded off a massive trailer parked nearby. A group of men are just finishing hammering together a ramp for the horse to walk down.

'In America you need a lift for everything. Not here. Here we do everything with our hands,' JC remarks proudly.

'You don't want to get on the wrong side of these guys,' he continues, nodding towards the group of big muscular Boers helping to unload the truck.

'That's why Americans are so fat,' he says.

Then he looks down at his own belly and adds: 'We're fat too, but that's because we're always with a beer in our hands.'

We laugh and there is no tension left in the quiet that follows.

But then JC asks: 'Do you know the word Kaffir, like nigger in America?'

And I shrink back. 'Yes.'

'Don't ever call a black man that to his face,' he says.

3

THE HUGO BROTHERS

Although he was the first to wish me welcome, Marius doesn't talk much. He tends the braai, cooking the meat over wood coals the way the Voortrekkers used to out on the veld. He serves drinks, grunting approvingly when he agrees with a comment someone makes. His in-laws, the Hugo brothers—Jacques, Carlo and Stefan—do most of the talking. They grew up on a farm among the Zulu people in KwaZulu-Natal and learned to speak Zulu even before they spoke Afrikaans. They would spend their days with Zulu children, making spears out of twigs and clay, running around, playing and swimming together.

'Our mother would call us home for supper, but most of the time we'd already eaten at the house of our Zulu friends. We'd have pap with sugar and milk, from the same pot as them,' Jacques recalls.

Jacques is a farmer and he and his wife live on their farm with eighty-four farm workers. He used to give his cattle herders ten cattle of their own in a herd of a hundred to motivate them to look after the animals well. The cattle herder would care for all the cattle, but use his own cattle for milk and to supplement his salary by selling the calves.

'Now, the government says that doesn't count as payment. It counts for nothing. But I'm not allowed to take the cattle back even though I've started paying minimum wage. I have two workers with the same positions who both get paid 1,600 rand a month, but one guy also has ten cattle while the other has none,' he tells me.

Then there are food and medical expenses, all adding up to a bill that has grown so steep Jacques claims it is hard to make ends meet.

'The workers live on the farm and plant there. I'm not allowed to kick workers off my farm since the government changed the law. Even if I lay off a worker, he and his family remain on the farm with their cattle and crops,' he says.

Jacques acknowledges that difference in culture is a problem, but he does not believe farmers are ignorant.

'Every farmer in Natal speaks at least three languages,' he says. 'People say there is racism because we don't understand one another or speak each other's languages. I'm fluent in Zulu. I grew up among Zulus. I still don't want to live among them.'

He notices my frown and asks: 'Do you know what it's like to watch when they skin their goats?'

I shake my head.

'They do it to please their forefathers. Do you know why they don't skin sheep?'

This time he doesn't wait for my reply.

'Because sheep don't make enough noise. The more noise the animal makes, the more it struggles and suffers, the happier their forefathers will be.'

He pauses for a moment, giving me time to digest his words. Then he continues: 'And there's no concept of planning. Any game you see you kill, right now, not caring about whether the animal is pregnant or whether you kill off all your sources of food.'

Jacques's younger brother, Stefan, is also a farmer. He has recently been to court four times for shooting the dogs used by poachers to kill game on his farm, but still no one has built a case against the poachers. Eventually the charges against him were dropped, but that was 10,000 rand in legal fees later. He now works extra as a teacher to make ends meet and, ironically, teaches maths to the young poachers who killed his game.

Both he and the third brother, Carlo, who is a full-time teacher, talk about the difficulties in teaching classes to pupils with such diverse cultures and backgrounds.

'Their skills sets and ways of thinking are so different from ours. In Zulu there are 2,000 shades of colour. They have over 2,000 ways of describing cattle that to us look all the same. In a herd of 500 cattle, a Zulu can immediately tell which one is missing without having to count them,' claims Carlo, though I remain sceptical.

According to Jacques, the relationship between farmers and their farm workers has deteriorated in recent years. Jacques believes that this is because of all the unfulfilled promises the government has given the poor.

'The government is making promises it can't keep; promises of free electricity, water and divisions of land that haven't been delivered on,' he says.

Jacques also feels that government officials aren't doing their jobs and that they are discriminating against the Afrikaners. But he is prepared for life in South Africa, even if all fails.

'This is my country. I'm not going anywhere,' he tells me.

'So what have you done to prepare yourself?' I ask.

'Do you want me to cover that in two minutes? That's books and books of plans. It covers everything from telecommunications to childbirth. Women will still give birth. We still have to be able to communicate and reach one another,' he says.

Jacques is far from the only Afrikaner with elaborate emergency plans, or what is commonly referred to as 'Plan B'. He belongs to the Suidlanders, an organisation founded in 2006 on the belief that, at any moment, a revolution could erupt in South Africa, precipitating chaos and anarchy. While the Suidlanders believe the revolution will start with black-on-black violence, they fear that aggression will quickly focus on white people, hence the need for safe havens. In preparation for this, the Suidlanders have developed incredibly elaborate evacuation plans, with secret locations having been created as safe zones. I'm told the infrastructure for food and food preparation is in place, as well as both national and global communications systems, and means of self-defence.

When I call Steve Meyer, head of the Suidlanders in Durban, he confirms Jacques's story: 'There are farm murders and blackouts. The police, education, road structure, everything is falling apart and the government has no answer. This has started pushing the masses towards action. There will be a political struggle and we won't be able to resolve it, so we are focusing on getting our people ready for evacuation. We don't have any violent tendencies. We're just concerned about our people. We'll go into hiding and stay there unless attacked. The UN will have to send help.'

The Suidlanders claim to have about 800,000 members, 650,000 of which are slotted into different structures for the evacuation. The remaining 150,000 are anonymous members who supposedly hold 'sensitive positions' in society. These figures cannot be confirmed and many believe them to be highly exaggerated, as it would mean that almost a third of South Africa's Afrikaner population of three million are members.

Carlo is less paranoid and his Plan B is proportionately less elaborate. Like most rural Afrikaners, he has a dog for protection. He also stores extra fuel and boxes of canned food in his garage. And he always fills up his car before returning home, so that he has enough petrol to escape should he need to.

One day when he and his family came home, the dog didn't rush to greet them like he usually does. Carlo immediately turned around and drove to Jacques's house. They left the women there, picked up some rifles, and returned by themselves. They quickly located the dog and discovered that everything was fine.

'But when you've seen what they do, especially to the women, you don't want to risk it,' he says. 'How do you live with yourself if something happened to your wife or daughter because you got sloppy and didn't take the right precautions? It's not that I expect the worst ... or I guess maybe I do ... You start to mistrust everyone.'

16 DECEMBER 1866

THE RIVER TO REST

In 1838, after the their victory at Blood River, the Voortrekkers founded Pietermaritzburg on the site the Zulu people called Umgungundlovu. Named after their leader Piet Retief, who had been slain by Dingaan, Pietermaritzburg was proclaimed capital of the newly created Republic of Natalia.

Here, the Voortrekkers began to collect funds and materials for the construction of the promised church in order to fulfil their vow to God. By the end of 1840, the church was completed, and in March 1841, the first service was held.

The building served as a church for nearly twenty years, until it was deemed too small for the size of the congregation. A new place of worship was constructed and the Church of the Vow was converted into a private school and rented out to other religious denominations.

In 1866, a ceremony was organised at the battle site. Many Afrikaners who had participated in the Great Trek in the 1830s attended, as did an old Zulu soldier who had fought in the battle. Each person present placed a stone at the site of the battle, erecting a cairn as a memorial. The ceremony was described by historians as a powerful symbol of early reconciliation. After 1866, 16 December was largely forgotten and few commemorated the date.[1]

In 1873, the Church of the Vow was sold. A firm of blacksmiths and wagon-makers purchased it and used it for their business for many years. Later it became a pharmacy.

4

THE NEW HOMELAND, ORANIA

'We would like to live as we once lived, but history will not permit it.'

John F Kennedy,
Remarks at the Breakfast of the Fort Worth Chamber of Commerce, 1963

In the early 1990s, one group of Afrikaners took their preparations for Armageddon a step further. When apartheid laws had been scrapped and Nelson Mandela was released from jail, they figured that merely stocking up on canned foods and ammunition wasn't going to cut it. So they followed the path of their forefathers, the Voortrekkers, and set out in search of a place to form their own republic—a place where they could live according to their values and control their destiny.

My acquaintances in Johannesburg dislike talking about Orania. When I insist, their answers are dismissive: 'They're into child labour,' someone tells me; 'They're a bunch of racists with their own flag and their own currency, trying to form their own republic,' someone else comments. Strong opinions abound, but it's those with the strongest opinions who haven't actually been there.

And when I ask Mark, his answer is terse, but definitive: 'I wouldn't be welcome. They'd call me a *Kafferboetie*, [a white person who has black friends]' he says.

29

BRIDGE OVER BLOOD RIVER

Persuading someone to accompany me on a visit to Orania proves difficult. It's a long drive to the middle of nowhere.

* * *

There is a reason nobody speaks of the interior route from Joburg to Orania as a 'scenic route'. Just west of Bloemfontein the arid highveld meets the equally arid Karoo region. The scenery is rocky and the Orange River half empty, but in the places where the land is cut open, blood-red soil emerges revealing that, in spite of the surface, with some irrigation these could be fertile lands.

I stop for the night in Bloemfontein and continue on an additional four-hour drive directly west the following morning. A few kilometres outside of Bloemfontein, towards Koffiefontein, the Lord appears to have run out of green paint, and arguably out of interest. The landscape flattens. The soil reddens. The vegetation yellows. The roads crumble back into the earth. The drive gets so monotonous that I start to think the car-sized potholes and untarred stretches of road are safety features: misguided efforts to keep people awake at the wheel.

Dust swirls up around the car. I'm surrounded by absolute drought. My GPS tells me I'm nearly there. And sure enough, a small town appears out of nowhere: a desert chameleon blending in perfectly with its surroundings. With the help of irrigation, vegetation is persuaded to return. Lush trees rise up from the ground to line the hard shoulder of the road and green grass softens its edges. A four-way stop marks the entrance to the town. A restaurant. A petrol station. A few quiet shops. If the middle of nowhere had a heart, this would be it.

I turn left and am greeted by a sign welcoming me to Orania and the offices of the Orania Movement, which according to their website aims to 'restore Afrikaner freedom in an independent, democratic republic based on Christian values and a healthy balance between independence and cooperation with surrounding areas.'

'It all started with eleven people. Now the population is just under a thousand,' says John Strydom, Director of Public Relations and my first point of contact in Orania.

We make our way to the nearby café and restaurant, where an overweight blond woman takes our order. Her skin is pinkish and her eyebrows and eyelashes so fair they're nearly invisible. Pizza, burgers and fried food dominate the menu. Vegetables have never been popular in the Afrikaner diet and people sometimes joke that chicken is considered a vegetable.

I order a cup of coffee and turn to Strydom.

'The idea, as such, is sixty years old,' he tells me. 'To have an area where you can be the majority, have your own institutions, and do your own work, rather than abusing other people without giving them voting rights. That is one of the most important cornerstones.'

Strydom is a stern-looking man who doesn't smile much, but somehow he still manages to come across as likeable. Throughout our conversation, he keeps returning to the notion of self-reliance, clearly considered a core virtue in Orania.

'This concept of *kafferwerk*, of having someone else do your work for you, is totally wrong. That is worse than any other form of political apartheid. Someone who works with his hands should be well paid and respected. But in a country where labour is cheap and abundant, that can often be a difficult transition.'

* * *

H.F. Verwoerd, Prime Minister of South Africa from 1958 until his assassination in 1966, always believed that if forced to choose between being rich and integrated or poor and segregated, the Afrikaners would choose the latter. But during apartheid most Afrikaners grew accustomed to the wealth and trappings of modern life built on the back of cheap black labour. To live separately in a homeland of their own, white people would have to get their own hands dirty. Few were prepared to do so.[1]

Then, in 1990, Verwoerd's son-in-law, Professor Carel Boshoff, and a group of Afrikaner families purchased a ghost town on the banks of the Orange River from the Department of Water Affairs. First established in the 1960s to house workers building irrigation canals to the Northern Cape farmland, Orania had been abandoned for nearly a decade and was starting to crumble. The founders and their families swiftly began building and renovating houses, planting neat gardens and transforming the old town into an Afrikaner community with all the necessary accoutrements of a homeland for 'good whites'.[2/3]

While Mandela was allegedly disappointed that these modern Voortrekkers did not believe in, nor wish to participate in, the building of the rainbow nation, the new government made room in the new constitution for the notion of a Boer state. In 1995, Mandela even flew in to visit the inhabitants of Orania, referred to by *The New York Times* as 'apartheid die-hards'. They greeted him politely and said they'd love to see him as president ... of a neighbouring country. The media cracked a few jokes about this group of mad men, but they were soon forgotten; left to themselves in their isolation.

Carel Boshoff IV, President of the Orania Movement and Chairman of the Board of Directors, is the grandson of Verwoerd (considered the architect of apartheid) and son of the founder of Orania, Professor Carel Boshoff III. When Carel Boshoff III passed away in March 2011, Carel Boshoff Jr was left the bearer of the ideological torch of Orania. I meet him at the same local café where I have just had my meeting with Strydom.

At forty-eight, Carel Boshoff can hardly be considered junior anymore. His blond hair is starting to recede and his light-blue eyes are framed by wrinkles as they rest behind a set of small circular spectacles, the trademark of the intellectual elite to which he belongs.

'A people is one generation deep,' he says. 'If one generation rejects itself, you are lost.'

According to Boshoff, Afrikaners realise that perennial control is an impossibility in an environment where they are not the majority.

'Most have accepted disintegration and become multicultural. Ethnic identity moves down the list of priorities until it's nowhere to be found,' he says, going on to quote a recent study showing that Afrikaners rate things like safety, freedom from crime, and material wealth at the top of their list of priorities. Cultural identity is only number eight or nine on the list.

The Orania Movement claims that the Afrikaner population is shrinking, while its average age is increasing. In addition, Afrikaners are widely spread out across the country. Orania is a radical response to this perceived threat of assimilation and cultural dilution. A minority can always become a majority through isolation. But the level of support required for a middle-class family to give up the trappings of modern society, pack up, and come to a place like Orania out in the middle of nowhere, is so extreme that Boshoff compares it to terrorism. I'm told that most Afrikaners aren't that radical.

I ask Boshoff about the ultimate aim of Orania. He says that freedom is a goal vague enough to be suitable: 'The experience of being able to manage your own affairs. The more freedom that can be secured for the Afrikaner, the closer Orania becomes to realising that goal. The core being that the Afrikaner is able to make decisions and act on them.'

When our meeting ends, I remain at the café, taking in my new surroundings. At the petrol station across from the parking lot, a car of black South Africans pulls up. A white attendant steps out to serve them. Then, a few minutes later, another car with black passengers stops to fill up. It takes me a few seconds to understand the profound implications of this scene for a country like South Africa. This is the first time since I arrived that I have seen a white person serving a black person. Jobs like cleaning, gardening, waiting tables and pumping petrol are almost always carried out by black people. Although I'm sure exceptions exist, Orania is the last place I expected to witness it given the town's reputation. It fits so well with the point Strydom was trying to make earlier that it almost feels orchestrated. That said, many things about Orania feel staged.

After lunch I wander over to the little grocery store to stock up on food, as Strydom has informed me that nothing will be open the following day, a Sunday. In addition to groceries, the shelves carry Afrikaans music and a small selection of books, including collections of first Bible stories for children. The speakers blast Afrikaans folk music on repeat. People are happy and cheerful, stopping to chat with one another and even with me.

When I pay I receive my first piece of Orania currency—a ten Ora bill. The note depicts the symbol of Orania: a little boy rolling up the sleeves of his orange shirt, ready to get to work. It also has a picture of Racheltjie de Beer, a teenage heroine who gave her own life saving her younger brother. The striking image symbolises the strength and tenacity of Afrikaner women, particularly during the Great Trek and the Boer Wars or Vryheidsoorloë (Freedom Wars).

The Ora comes in 10, 20, 50 and 100 denominations. The bills have the watermarks of normal paper bills, but are printed on thicker paper, making them feel more like coupons than actual money. The currency has become a powerful symbol of independence, but also serves to enhance local economic development. It works like this: residents of Orania deposit their rands at the bank and in return they receive an equal amount of Ora. Ora are then used for transactions within the community. You receive your salary in Ora and pay for your goods and services in Ora. For every Ora in the system there must be a rand in the bank. The accumulated interest on all the rands in the bank is then used for community development, such as getting Internet to Orania. Locals say they like having their own currency as it adds to the feeling of security. There is little point in robbing an Oranian: outside of Orania, the Ora is as worthless as Monopoly money.

The community is built on private land owned by the Orania Company. However, the goal is to become a separate republic or at least some sort of federation. Homeowners are shareholders of the company. There are currently around four hundred share-holders who vote for a board of directors. There is also a repre-sentative council that is elected by all residents.

The residents of Orania pay their national tax to the South African government but municipal tax and property tax to the Orania Company. Budget authority rests with the company. The company collects taxes and spends them on service delivery. However, not all services are available within city limits. To visit the hospital, for example, residents must travel the 43 km to Hopetown.

Financial viability and sustainability are two important priori-ties of the council, as they directly relate to the community's long-term survival. Having one's economic affairs in order is also a key part of the Afrikaner value system. Over the past twenty years, the budget has risen fifteen per cent a year on average. From 2010 to 2011, revenues rose by fifty per cent.

To become a resident of Orania one must pass an admission interview with Strydom and the rest of the town council.

'We try to make sure people are coming for the right reasons, not just fleeing,' he says.

The 'right' reasons are generally related to the desire to preserve Afrikanerdom: Afrikaner culture, language, and traditions.

'Identity is not politically correct anymore. There's this con-cept of one-size-fits-all. So people come here looking for the last outpost of apartheid or for tension between us and the government,' Strydom tells me.

Although preferable, having Afrikaner blood in your veins is not a prerequisite. There is a German who has been living in Orania for fifteen years, but he knew the language and culture well when he arrived. There are also Afrikaners who have arrived with British spouses. But there are no black or Coloured residents.

'Could a person of colour, who speaks Afrikaans, embraces the Afrikaner culture and is married to an Afrikaner, become a resident?' I ask Boshoff.

'It is not theoretically impossible, but it would be very difficult,' he replies.

'I've worked alongside enough people of different ethnicities to understand that it can happen. I've met enough attractive and intelligent people to understand how it could happen. But the idea that by way of romantic love you transcend and bridge cultural differences is not true. A common frame of reference can be sacrificed, but it has its price. I am critical of the notion that personal value is higher than communal value.'

But, at the same time, Boshoff maintains that Orania is not anti-black: 'If that's what you are after, you are probably in the wrong place. This is not just about race. It's a cultural marker; it's about historic division. Many whites wanted to close the book on race, but they are constantly reminded of it by the blacks,' he says.

'There have been blacks who have contacted us saying they want to come for the resident's interview. We tell them to come, but no one has ever showed up. We've had plenty of jokers, but so far no one serious,' Strydom adds.

Right now, Orania's expansion is limited by a lack of housing. Having a place to live and a way to make a living is a prerequisite for becoming a resident. However, more land was recently acquired and eight construction companies are busy planning and putting up more houses.

THE NEW HOMELAND, ORANIA

With the recent purchase of an adjacent farm, the Orania Company now owns just over 7,000 hectares of land. Agriculture is the primary industry. There are 16,000 pecan trees in Orania; a hundred tons of pecans were exported to China in the first half of 2012. Other crops include everything from lettuce, to almonds and olives. To facilitate irrigation, expansion is taking place alongside the Orange River.

Manie Opperman, chairman of the town council, drives me out to look at the new land.

If the current growth rate persists, Orania will have a population of 20,000 people in eighteen years. Growing faster than that would require outside support and investment.

'Modern society requires a lot of people. The ideal would be a community of between 300,000 and 500,000 Afrikaners, living in balance with the surrounding people and able to survive as a cultural group with its own identity in Africa,' Opperman says.

As we arrive, a group of men on the banks of the river are busy surveying how to best divide it up into lots for houses. I thought I was meeting the chairman in an office environment. As such, I am dressed in black suit pants and high-heeled boots. Opperman, dressed comfortably in his casual farm wear, seems amused at my clumsy progress down to the river.

We conduct our entire interview standing on the muddy banks of the river. Why take a seat in the shade under the nearby tree when one can stand erect and absorb the full heat of the African sun? Opperman is a man of the soil; a man who has worked hard his whole life. His hands, his weathered face, his firm posture all testify to that. Whether you are part of Orania's intellectual elite, like he is, or an unskilled farm labourer, you mustn't be afraid to work hard and get your hands dirty. Orania is 'no place for sissies', according to the community's unofficial motto.

'You must be a jack of all trades, a generalist, to make it in Orania,' says Opperman. 'The people who thrive here often arrive as a family: grandparents, children, everyone.'

Now, twenty years after its founding, the people of Orania are still very much pioneers and have to be prepared to live without many of the comforts of modern society.

So why come?

While there is a lot of talk about cultural and linguistic identity among the intellectual elite of Orania, the more people I meet, the more it seems that fear has been the primary motivator for most who have relocated here.

When I ask Opperman how many of the people who come to Orania have been victimised by crime, he says that no statistics are kept, but that his perception is that most have been. He tells me that he recently participated in a group interview with eleven Afrikaners seeking residency—all of them had been victims of crime.

Opperman, for his part, has had twelve attacks on his own immediate family, including one murder. His son, a civil engineer, was attacked at a construction site by eight men. He was beaten until near death. His daughter was attacked and robbed on a farm. His brothers and his uncle have also been victims of violence.

While there are no barbed wires or security fences in Orania, about twenty volunteers take turns patrolling the area around the clock. If anything serious happens, the police station in Hopetown is contacted. But like most places in South Africa, there is little faith in the police. In order to minimise this external dependence, a private security company is being established in Orania, with a core group of enthusiastic locals being put through professional security training. Presently, its isolated location and lack of wealth are the community's best defence.

'We are far from everything, too small to attract attention and not rich enough to rob,' says Strydom.

Nor is the community interested in accumulating wealth, as they believe this would make them a target.

'Fortunately we haven't found any diamonds here. If we did we would probably put them back in the ground and cover them again,' someone comments.

It seems people have not forgotten that it was the discovery of minerals that caused the Anglo-Boer Wars and first challenged Afrikaner self-determination a century ago.

But Opperman is careful to point out that he is not afraid.

'I've been to war. I've seen people die. We are good soldiers. There is no reason why we shouldn't be able to fight if we have to,' he says.

For Opperman, like most of Orania's intellectual elite, the greatest fear is not victimisation, but assimilation.

'After World War Two, Algeria had three million white French. They are all gone. The Belgians who used to live in the Congo are all gone. The Portuguese are gone. The English are gone. The Afrikaners are the last European people remaining in Africa ...' He emphasises this last statement.

My scepticism going unnoticed, he continues: 'This is because we had all those years between 1960 and 1991 to establish a Western economic system and development. You can't just destroy a people anymore, so we have an opportunity if we are clever. We have to bring more people here. Otherwise assimilation is inevitable. If your cultural framework is gone you lose direction and hope.'

According to Opperman, the loss of power destabilised the Afrikaner culture and spurred an identity crisis.

'We've lost control over the universities, the military, and the economy; over all aspects of society that enable you to determine the course in which you develop. Now it's all in the hands of the ANC. The ANC has almost 70 per cent of the vote. There is massive corruption. The school system has been destabilised by new curriculums, brought in for good reasons but not properly executed. It all seems to be about placing guilt on our children because they have received better treatment over the years than the African people.'

The children of Orania, however, appear free from guilt. It's an October weekend in 2011. School is out. I find the local youth by following the sound of laughter and shrieks all the way to the community recreation centre. There is an inviting swimming pool surrounded by lush grass, picnic tables and braai pits. I'm immediately taken aback by the postcard perfection of it all: married couples, hand-in-hand, watch their toddlers splash around in the kiddies' pool, while the older children laugh and play, their athletic, tanned, young bodies skipping and jumping. Someone initiates a rugby game and all join in: boys and girls of all ages. The older boys show amazing patience with the feeble attempts of the little ones, and when a little girl gets hurt the game stops and the older girls rush to comfort her and make sure she's okay before the play resumes. No fights. No bullying. They are almost nauseatingly happy, well adjusted and well behaved. All laughter and fun in the sun. I feel like I'm in Stepford, the idyllic town in Ira Levin's novel *The Stepford Wives*, where the women turn out to be robots, with their husbands behind the remote controls. Amazed, I look for the hidden cameras.

As I walk back from the pool to my guesthouse, I realise I haven't walked much since I arrived in South Africa. Except for in Cape Town, there is hardly any infrastructure to support pedestrians, and few white people seem to consider it safe to wander about on foot. Having arrived in Orania from Johannesburg, via Bloemfontein, the contrast is stark. No fences, no razor wire. One can actually see each of the pretty little houses and admire their perfectly laid out gardens. In the fields surrounding the community, people play rugby and *jukskei*. Signs on the roads warn passersby to watch out for toddlers on tricycles.

* * *

Before arriving in Orania I tried to find a local family to stay with, but to no avail. According to Strydom, quite a few locals felt let down after opening their homes to journalists. Now many are sceptical and reluctant to talk. So I'm staying at ChaDuBri, a little guesthouse run by Lottie. But, as the guesthouse is in fact Lottie's home, and there are currently no other guests, I'm happy with the arrangement.

Lottie is the perfect Afrikaner matron. Though I don't dare to ask her age, I guess she is in her early sixties. She is still stunningly beautiful, with blonde hair and clear blue eyes. No matter how early in the morning, I always find her well dressed, with carefully applied make-up, waiting in the kitchen ready to serve me an elaborate breakfast of eggs prepared in various ways, sausages, bacon, yoghurt parfaits and scones. And for dessert, there are *koeksisters*—twists of deep-fried dough soaked in syrup.

The inside of her home is as neatly kept as the outside. The furniture is of a rustic, country style, complete with lavish sofas, solid wooden tables, and beautifully made cushions and duvets crafted by Lottie's equally beautiful daughter. Over the generous fireplace rest family pictures: Lottie with her children and her late husband.

Lottie has been living in Orania for two and a half years. She used to live in Winburg in the Free State where she and her husband had a farm, the same farm where he was once born. They were married for forty years before he died of cancer. Lottie stayed on at the farm for a while with her son, but fear eventually got the better of her.

During her last years at the farm, she witnessed her share of atrocities. First, the family next door was brutally murdered.

'They killed everyone: father, mother, daughter and granddaughter,' she tells me.

Then another neighbour, whom Lottie refers to as 'the bachelor', was murdered while in the process of moving from his farm. And, finally, a third neighbour suffered a vicious attack on their estate when the wife, but not the husband, was killed.

'My son didn't want to leave me alone on the farm anymore and I felt that this was starting to interfere with his life,' she says.

Lottie also wanted a new beginning in a place where not everything reminded her of her late husband. As her daughter had already moved from Pretoria to Orania, to be able to give her children a 'rural and carefree childhood' just like the one she had, Lottie decided to follow suit. Lottie now has three grand-daughters in Orania whom she takes care of in the mornings while her daughter, Celeste, is at work.

Lottie describes Orania as a bit of a 'man's world', where more women are needed.

'Because men initiated the project they still feel like they deserve all the say,' she says and adds that everyone seems to expect women to create their own job opportunities, simply 'invent their own thing' in order to make a living.

Lottie tries to be creative. Immediately after her arrival she started her guesthouse. For the past three months she has also been running a little clothing store from her garage. But business is slow and the guesthouse log shows an average of only one booking per month.

'You pretty much have to live off savings,' Lottie says.

Lottie employs two women who take turns to help her at the guesthouse. She also has a man who helps her in the garden once a week. Having white servants was hard at first, she tells me.

'I wasn't used to working with white people, but now it's fine. It's easier to teach them things because I understand how they think. And they are more reliable,' she says.

Lottie imagines that in the beginning it must have been very hard for them to be servants.

'But then again they are not treated like servants, not really. They are more treated like help than servants,' she says.

Lottie confides that she is proud to be an Afrikaner: 'We are a unique group of people. We are pioneers. We are steady people with integrity who work hard.'

At this, Lottie's friend Nikolas, who has been sitting quietly on the sofa while Lottie and I talk, frowns. He is a 'hardcore' Afrikaner. The kind who will reluctantly greet you in English the first time he meets you, but who refuses to do it again as he feels that by the second encounter you ought to have picked up enough Afrikaans to return the courtesy.

The first time I saw Nikolas he was busy working in the garden. I assumed he was the gardener. But after having bumped into him at the house early in the morning and then again late at night, I no longer know what to think. At least by now I know better than to ask. In Orania, not even people of Lottie's age are allowed 'sleepovers' unless they are married, and for me to ask questions that would insinuate in any way that the two might be romantically involved would be considered highly offensive.

Yet, the topic of work ethics is apparently engaging enough for Nikolas to make an exception to his rule of no English. In his strong accent, and with a fair bit of help from Lottie, he explains that he used to have his own business but went into farming instead because 'the sheep don't talk back' and because they 'multiply while you sleep'. He has little faith in the ability of any worker, white or black.

'They are statues!' he exclaims.

'Who?'

'The gardeners outside the offices of the Orania Movement.'

'You mean Fransie?' I ask. With so few people roaming the streets it doesn't take long to know exactly who is who.

'Oh, I don't know their names, but they just stand around,' Nikolas replies.

'People like them are looked after here,' Lottie intercepts. 'It depends on them what they do with it.'

16 DECEMBER 1881

THE RISE OF AFRIKANER NATIONALISM

'Legend: A lie that has attained the dignity of age.'

H.L. Mencken

It was the republican Afrikaner leader Paul Kruger who initiated the first efforts to resurrect the spirit of the Battle of Blood River. Sensing the great symbolic potential of the battle, he proceeded to turn the Great Trek into a heroic myth emphasising the Afrikaners' passion for freedom and will to survive as an independent people against overwhelming odds. Afrikaner victories were used to shape the story of a golden age.[1]

The British had allowed the Trekboers to head inland from the Cape unharmed, establishing independent Boer republics such as Natalia, the Orange Free State and the Transvaal. These hardy pioneers served as trailblazers, battling the indigenous populations and opening up the frontier for others to follow.

In the Boer republics, the Voortrekkers were free to rule the black population according to their strict religious beliefs. While the smaller mini-states were short-lived, the Orange Free State and the Transvaal lasted decades, even recognised by European powers as independent countries. But all of this changed when diamonds were discovered in Kimberley in 1869. By 1877 the British had annexed all the Boer republics, save the Orange Free State. The Afrikaners were of course incensed and, in 1880, the first Anglo-Boer War, or War of Independence, broke out. The Afrikaners chose their symbolic date of the Blood River victory—16 December—to declare the Transvaal independent and fire the first rounds that sparked the war.

Although they were badly outnumbered and had no formal military training, they exploited their superior knowledge of the terrain and expert marksmanship to swiftly defeat the British. The ensuing peace agreement saw the formation of the Zuid-Afrikaansche Republiek, the South African Republic or ZAR, which secured Boer self-governance in domestic affairs.

On 16 December 1881, Kruger spoke at a state festival, organised by the Transvaal government, to commemorate the Battle of Blood River, as well as the recent victory over the British. In his speech he compared Afrikaners to the Israelites of the Old Testament—a people of God, fighting both black and white enemies to achieve their Promised Land. The history of South Africa became the history of the brave Afrikaner taking a stand against both British imperialism and black barbarism. Anything that did not fit within this nationalist narrative was ignored.

However, neither peace nor self-determination was long-lived. In 1886 an Australian miner named George Harrison discovered gold in the area around Johannesburg. Within ten years the miners' camp exploded into the largest city in South Africa as fortune seekers arrived from across the continent, and around the world, particularly from Britain. Kruger quickly recognised that if these so-called uitlanders were allowed to continue to immigrate to the republics, they would soon outnumber the Boers, and pose a threat to Boer self-determination, culture and language. When the true scale of the gold find became apparent, it once again awoke the mineral envy of the imperialist British, who used the issue of 'uitlander' rights to begin to amass troops near the borders. On 9 October 1899, the Boers gave the British 48 hours' notice to back down. The British refused and the Second Anglo-Boer War erupted. While the Boers started strongly, the British sent significant reinforcements until they outnumbered the Afrikaners five to one. The British quickly took control of the cities, but the Afrikaners proved both stubborn and resilient in the rural areas, relying on guerrilla tactics to wear the British down.

To crush the resistance of the Afrikaners, the British deployed a scorched earth policy, systematically destroying farms, slaughtering cattle and putting women and children in concentration camps, as they pushed the Boers deeper into the veld. 26,000 Afrikaners, most of them children, died of disease and neglect in the camps. This suffering eventually broke the spirit of the Afrikaners, who surrendered in 1902 after having fought the first anti-colonial war of the twentieth century.[2] One of the first peoples to experience the horrors of concentration camps, it would take generations and a new common enemy for many Afrikaners to forgive the British. One can still, to this day, score quick social points with a well-placed jab at the English.

With the peace accord came the promise of democratic self-determination, an offer made much easier by the sheer number of British colonists now in the region. But the Afrikaners had paid a heavy price for freedom. The war had left them devastated and when the Union of South Africa was established on 31 May 1910, most of its poor whites were Afrikaners.

5

THE NEW TREK

'What must I feed Nancy?' Charna turns to her father.

'Ag, give her some bread.'

Charna sighs and gets up. On the kitchen table rests a chipped plate with a piece of meat left over from yesterday's dinner. It has been sitting unrefrigerated on the kitchen table all day long, so no one will eat it. Charna adds it to the plate of sliced bread and goes outside.

'Nancy! Nancy! I have food for you!' she shouts.

Nancy emerges from the shed to fetch the plate of food. She eats in the shade, and then falls asleep. It is 5 pm. Nancy is the family's live-in maid.

Charna is a blonde and blue-eyed South African I met ten years previously on a European cruise ship. We partied in some of the harbours where the ship docked along the way. We had talked about deceitful sailors and about which bars served the best cocktails, but we had never talked about politics. It took a long time before I even realised that Afrikaans was her first language. I assumed her habit of starting each sentence with a long 'Jaaa ...' was something she had picked up from the rest of the crew, which consisted mainly of Scandinavians. I found her on

Facebook and, after a few short emails back and forth, I decided to visit her at her parents' farm in the Transkei to learn more about everyday life for South Africa's white farmers.

* * *

My first night at the house is restless. I sleep lightly and wake up to the sound of loud clicks. It's Charna's father, Peter, chatting away to Nancy in Xhosa, South Africa's second most widely-spoken language (the first is Zulu).

I find them in the kitchen as I go in search of breakfast. The clicks increase in both frequency and volume, betraying Peter's growing agitation. Clearly failing to get his message across, he switches to English and then to Afrikaans. I soon discern that Nancy has been given the job of reorganising the cupboards. She is busy moving cups and plates around. Meanwhile a frustrated Peter is failing, in all three languages, to explain how he wants it done. Finally, he moves Nancy gently aside and proceeds to do it himself.

'It's hard to find good help these days,' he says as he tasks her with sweeping the kitchen floors instead. 'But what can we do? She has nowhere else to go.'

Nancy is moving the dirt around in circles with her broom. She speaks decent English, so I'm surprised when Peter turns to me and continues to speak as though she isn't there.

'They had it better before, you know. And most of them will tell you so. At least back then they would get their pensions on time and things worked.'

'Are you and Charna going to the beach today?' he continues in a lighter tone. The crease on his forehead vanishes as he changes topics.

'Yes, I think so. If the weather stays nice.'

'Well, you must go early. We used to have this beach to ourselves but now they are everywhere: crowding the place, playing their music. But you mustn't let it get to you. You must just go early. They are lazy. They won't be there before 11 am. They love to sleep. Just go first thing in the morning.'

Nancy keeps moving her broom, and the dust it has collected, round and round. If his words upset her, her face does not betray it.

When Peter is done organising the cupboard, he makes Nancy a cup of tea with plenty of sugar and sends her off to rest. A few minutes later, Charna enters the kitchen.

'Charna, would you mind sweeping up the floor?' Peter asks, rhetorically.

Charna sighs but gets started. After years working in the cruise ship industry, she is no stranger to manual labour. She was happy there, but after the captain knocked her up and left her, she returned home to her parents in South Africa.

'So what is life around here like?' I ask.

'Ag, it's nice. But … it has become very black,' she whispers. 'They are everywhere now.'

Charna is not too happy about being home. Nor is she very optimistic about her prospects of ever leaving again. As a single mom with an illegitimate child her dating options in the conservative Afrikaner community are limited.

When the baby was born the captain came to visit. Her dad did his best to persuade him to acknowledge his responsibility and start a family with Charna. But the captain never returned. All Peter can do now is praise the Lord that at least the child isn't Coloured. He is a blond and blue-eyed little rugby player who helps his grandpa care for the animals on the farm.

Peter has chickens, goats, horses, sheep and pigs. He used to have cows as well, but gave that up as he felt he couldn't rely on his workers. On the many days when no one showed up, he would have to milk the cows himself—a 12-hour job. Even now, without the cows, it's hard for him to leave the farm overnight, but at least he can manage the animals he has on his own. As if to prove his point, that evening none of his workers arrive, and I follow Peter around as he feeds and tends to the animals while cursing his staff through his teeth.

Walking the idyllic fields that surround the family farm, it's hard to imagine that farm work is South Africa's most dangerous occupation.[1] Twice as many farm workers as police officers are killed each year and someone working on a farm is almost four times more likely to be murdered than the average South African.[2]

For the 200 years preceding the fall of apartheid, South African farms operated like throwbacks to feudal times, but with a racial twist: a white, land-owning master, commanding, and supposedly protecting, a workforce of black serfs. Black workers, frequently born on the farm, were typically given small patches of land to live on and tend to for their own needs while working the feudal lord's plot. While not all white farmers mistreated their workers, stories of atrocities are so common as to make it difficult not to generalise. The fear of losing land to the vastly larger black population seemed to inspire a 'rule with an iron fist' approach to management among many Afrikaners. Missing items, 'cheekiness', tardiness and other perceived wrongdoings were frequently met with violence, destruction of the workers' huts or property, and eviction; the latter considered the most devastating as it meant not only the end of the ability to meet the subsistence needs of the family, but the severance of identity with the land they had always known.

As apartheid began to crumble, the violence began to swing increasingly in the other direction, escalating as time passed. Since 1990, more than a thousand white commercial farmers have been murdered in South Africa, according to the Transvaal Agricultural Union of South Africa (TAU SA). In the same time period, sixty black farmers were murdered on their farms, according to TAU SA.[3]

The high murder rate has the commercial farming community of roughly 35,000 people deeply concerned.

In 2011, the trade union Solidarity and TAU SA published a book called *Land of Sorrow*, which listed all verifiable farm attacks since 1991. Each of the close to three thousand incidents receives only a sentence or two, but it still makes for more than three hundred pages of gruesome reading: bludgeonings, tortures, rapes.

'I just don't feel safe staying here anymore. It makes me uncomfortable,' says Charna.

Although she grew up on this farm, in the last ten years, things have changed. Recently a neighbour was attacked and brutally beaten. Every farmer knows a farmer who has been killed.

While the family hasn't directly experienced any attacks involving violence, they have had a few break-ins by farm workers.

'One guy I was about to lay off anyway. He beat me to it,' says Peter who claims that a little 'roughing up' with an iron rod was all it took for the guy to confess he was the one behind the break-in.

Peter rode with him in the back of a bakkie all the way to the police station and beat him for revenge.

'You don't want to see this,' he told the officers up front who left him to it.

'Didn't the guy try to defend himself?' I ask.

'No, he didn't dare to,' Peter replies.

But that was almost ten years ago now. That kind of vigilantism wouldn't be tolerated these days. And while most farmers are quick to tell you their workers are treated well and don't hold any grudges, the gruesome circumstances under which many farmers are tortured before being murdered makes it difficult to rule out the element of retaliation.

* * *

André Botha is president of the Gauteng division of the commercial farmers' association, AgriSA. He is also head of the association's Rural Safety Committee and holds a senior rank within the police reservists. As such, he is often one of the first to show up at the scene of a farm attack.

I ask him why he believes farm attacks are often characterised by so much violence, especially when there is frequently so little stolen.

'Often the violence involved is about getting information about safes, pin numbers, etcetera. Genetically Afrikaners are rebels. It's in our blood to defend ourselves. We're not afraid. If someone has no right to take something, we won't give it up without a fight,' he says.

Botha tells me the story of a farm attack he was called to just a few days earlier. The attackers broke into the farmhouse and tied up the farmer, demanding the pin code for his bank account. He refused. The attackers filled the kettle and put it on the stove. 'We will fill your ears with boiling water,' they told him. Still he refused. They waited for the water to boil, grabbed his head, and again demanded the code. Still he refused. Then, they slowly burnt out the flesh of his ear with boiling water. When they began to tilt his head the other way to start on the second ear, he relented and gave them the code. In the meantime, some of the burglars exploring the house had found another card.

'And this time, they poured boiling water on his genitals,' Botha says.

'Why didn't he just give them the code right away this time?' I ask.

Botha looks at me sternly: 'A Boer doesn't give anything up without a fight,' he replies.

In South Africa farms are often referred to as 'soft targets' because they are frequently isolated, far from immediate help. With police desperately short of resources, farmers work with local police to organise their own reserve patrols 24/7, 365 days a year. Reservists patrol in police uniforms using police cars. According to Botha, about fifty per cent of all South African commercial farmers are also reservists in the police.

Botha has a wife and three kids. He says he is not afraid, but always conscious of his surroundings, that 'anything else would be foolish.' He has a dog with him at all times.

'It will warn me if someone comes. Not taking protective measures and arming oneself would be stupid out here,' he says.

I meet Botha near his farm south of Johannesburg. He is busy helping a neighbouring farmer dissemble a massive planter and load it onto a big truck. It's December 2011 and, as we speak, a convoy of farmers are moving from South Africa to the Congo. Sixteen families from Botha's area have already started their journey north, up through Namibia and Angola, with their truckloads of equipment and possessions. Next month, another thirty families will follow.

In 2009, the government of the Republic of the Congo contacted AgriSA offering South African commercial farmers 200,000 hectares of arable land, with the possibility of an additional 10 million hectares at a later stage. Farmers received extendable thirty-year leases and tax exemptions.[4]

More than 50 per cent of the population of the Congo Republic is undernourished and living on less than two dollars a day, according to Human Development Reports from the United Nations.[5] Despite rich soils and extremely favourable farming conditions, the country spends billions each year on food imports, mainly from its former colonial landlord France, as most Congolese farmers are subsistence farmers who lack the necessary skills and technology to support commercial farming. South Africa, on the other hand, exports much of its produce despite most of its land being arid or semi-arid with low average rainfall, making crops vulnerable to drought.

When I speak to Dawie Maree, economist at AgriSA, he tells me that the general agricultural conditions of South Africa aren't very good: 'In the past few years there have been several droughts. There is very little farmers' support. Farmers have to compete against imported products from subsidised farmers in the EU and, to some extent, America,' he says.

Between 2002 and 2007, the number of South African commercial farmers declined from 60,000 to 40,000, according to Maree. Since 2001, the agriculture industry has shed more than 300,000 jobs across South Africa.[6]

Maree believes the lack of support will undermine any attempts at land reform: 'If a commercial farmer struggles, an emerging farmer will struggle even more. The government must help or we won't have any more farmers,' he says.

During apartheid the white minority owned 90 per cent of the arable land, in spite of the fact that they made up only 10 per cent of the population. When coming to power, the African National Congress (ANC) promised to transfer 30 per cent of South Africa's arable land to the previously disadvantaged majority by 2014.[7] But so far land redistribution has been unsuccessful. Though the numbers are contested, according to Africa Check less than 10 per cent of the promised land has been redistributed since the end of apartheid,[8] and the government has failed to provide the assistance needed to make the farms successful under their new owners.

'There is a certain image of owning land in the African culture; that if you own land you are rich. But just owning land makes you poor. You have to use the land. Some of the land reform beneficiaries don't want to farm, just to own land. The government must select those who want to and have the skills to farm,' says Maree.

He claims that members of AgriSA are jointly investing 80 million rand in the training of black emerging farmers, supplying them with white commercial farming mentors. The state-sanctioned land-grab in Zimbabwe has acted as a deterring example of what can happen if things aren't done right.

'There will come a stage where you will have to give something not to lose everything. The farmers of Zimbabwe have taught us that. We acknowledge that land reform must be done to prevent a situation like the one in Zimbabwe,' says Maree.

After all, Zimbabwean land reform also started out with the government buying farms from willing sellers. It wasn't until after years of failure to meet the land redistribution targets and a lack of funds, that President Robert Mugabe finally decided to sanction the land-grabs.

Still, there are increasing signs that this is where things are heading. To rectify their failure, the government has now abandoned the principle of 'willing seller, willing buyer'. They have also drafted new legislation enabling the state to expropriate without paying former owners full—or in some cases any—compensation.[9]

But, while the South African government keeps its white commercial farmers at arm's length, many other African nations regard their skills as a valuable asset with which to combat food scarcity. In addition to Republic of Congo, more than twenty other African nations have also reached out to South Africa's commercial farmers, many of whom are now on their way to places like Zambia, Ghana, Somalia, Namibia, Botswana and Angola. More than eight hundred families have already relocated to Mozambique. The next wave is heading to Sierra Leone and Uganda. The exodus is well underway.

Like modern Voortrekkers setting out on the Great Trek of the twenty-first century, Afrikaners are packing up their lives, loading their belongings onto trucks and slowly making their way across the continent. Escaping drought, economic strain, political uncertainty and violence, they are looking for a place to start anew.

16 DECEMBER 1912

THE RECONSTRUCTION OF THE AFRIKANER BEGINS

With defeat in the Second Anglo-Boer War came the loss of Afrikaner political power and economic capacity. However, as Afrikaners still made up the majority of South Africa's white population, it was feasible that they could rise again to dominate a new, unified South Africa. The intellectual elite knew the best way to achieve this was to forge a common identity; a renewed sense of pride. They began by resurrecting the most powerful symbols from their past.

The original Church of the Vow had been sold to private interests in 1873. Over the next forty years the building was used as a wagon maker's shop, a mineral water factory, a tearoom, a pharmacy, a blacksmith's shop and a wool shed, and was significantly altered a number of times. But in 1909, the Church Council of the local Dutch Reformed Church began a national campaign to raise funds for the repurchase of the church so that it could be preserved in honour of the Voortrekkers. The building was restored as close to its original form as possible and established as a museum exclusively for Voortrekker relics.

On 16 December 1912, the seventy-fourth anniversary of the Battle of Blood River, its doors opened once again to the white public.

6

GOOD WHITES, POOR WHITES

The destruction of Afrikaner farms during the Second Anglo-Boer War accelerated the process of natural urbanisation as destitute Afrikaners were forced to try to make a living in the cities. By the time the economic depression hit in the 1930s, nearly 50 per cent of Afrikaners were estimated to have been 'poor' or 'very poor'. In urban centres, members of the white, black and Coloured lower class began sharing quarters. Some Afrikaners even became domestic workers or farm workers for African and Coloured people.

For the Afrikaner elite working to rebuild Afrikaner pride, the situation was intolerable, and the potential ramifications for the *volk* unacceptable. The existence of poor, uneducated white people completely undermined the idea of a modern, industrial society premised on white superiority. But, like most diseases, so-called poor whiteism was thought to be curable. These genetically superior people simply needed to be provided with the right environment in order to fulfil their potential.

In the 1930s officials travelled to study model communities in England, Germany and Sweden, places where it was believed that the middle class enjoyed a suburban lifestyle of peaceful *gemeen-*

skap (community). It was thought that constructing similar suburbs, separated from the surrounding non-white areas, would minimise the threat of class-based alliances and miscegenation, while at the same time offering the opportunity to uplift poor whites through carefully structured social engineering.[1]

The first suburb was called Jan Hofmeyr, constructed in Johannesburg in 1936. Two years later, Epping Garden Village was established near Cape Town. Soon every South African town with a notable white population had at least one suburb focusing on the rehabilitation of poor whites.

These areas had to be designed so as to be easy to control. A neighbourhood would typically consist of a central open space surrounded by houses. A single entrance road would circle the central space and exit the same way. This made it easy to supervise who came and went.

Houses were designed to promote traditional family values. Everyone should have their own bed and there could be no more than three children per bedroom. After the age of seven, siblings of opposite genders were no longer allowed to share a bedroom. Parents also had to have their own bedroom. The use of space was strictly regulated so as to prevent potentially inappropriate situations.[2]

Specially trained professionals, such as social workers, teachers, doctors, and of course church personnel instructed residents on what attitudes they should adopt concerning work and the use of free time, cleanliness and health, morals and sexuality, bodily appearance and behaviour, social and racial relations, as well as family life.[3]

Couples had to be married or leave the suburb. Cohabitation of non-married couples was strictly prohibited. A solid family nucleus was the basis of a good white family. The police hunted down men who abandoned their families—not supporting your family was considered a criminal offence. Social workers monitored everything from residents' hygiene (good hygiene was seen as a prerequisite for happiness) down to the smallest details of their behaviour.[4]

Children had to be hardworking, neat and controlled. The inability to raise your children according to these standards could result in them being taken away and raised in institutions. Among some families, the values of 'good whiteism' had been so thoroughly internalised that parents would report their own children's shortcomings and voluntarily send them off to institutions to avoid having the family's record negatively affected.[5]

Gardens were seen as having endless benefits and every house had one. Gardening in the fresh air was considered constructive for both body and mind, and could help people develop a more sophisticated sense of aesthetics. A garden could also make it easier to lower household spending, as certain foods, particularly fruit and vegetables, could be self-cultivated. Thriving European-looking gardens also had significant symbolic value, as they were regarded as a triumph of European civilisation over the primitive wilderness of Africa. Yearly garden competitions were organised and the state of household gardens closely monitored. In 1946, 67 per cent of the families of Epping Garden Village had a well-kept garden, according to the records of the housing company.[6]

Each house would look out onto the houses of several neighbours, and fences were low or non-existent. That way people could keep an eye on each other and any inappropriate conduct would be noticed and reported. The only privacy was inside the houses, but even then one had to be prepared at all times for unannounced inspection visits from social workers or other professionals.[7]

When a family received a house, a social worker would visit to lay down the rules and enforce them until they had been internalised. It was not uncommon for a social worker to personally demonstrate the 'right way' to clean or organise a space. Those who failed to comply would face disciplinary measures. If structured home visits weren't enough, it was within the social worker's power to deny resources, have the children taken away, or recommend that the person be sent to a work colony or even a mental institution.

The authorities also decided what residents needed and how they were allowed to spend their money. They kept meticulous records of how much each family spent, and on what, and didn't hesitate to interfere with what they regarded as inappropriate purchases. In 1950, it was decided that only those residents of Epping Garden Village who needed a car for their work should be allowed to buy one.

This control even extended to the residents' free time. It was believed that keeping them busy with the 'right' kinds of hobbies, like gardening, sports and church activities, would ensure they stayed out of trouble. Leisure was largely divided along gender lines. Women were to take an interest in housework, childcare, sewing and decorating, while men were mostly directed towards sport and gardening.[8]

Being work-shy was considered the worst possible characteristic of any man. Women, on the other hand, were entirely judged on their appearance and ability to create a lovely home. The condition of the home was the most important way for a woman to demonstrate her moral capacity. Epping Garden Village archival documentation, such as the report extracts below,[9] illustrates how social workers would judge residents based on the neatness of their home:

> On different visits the house was found to be untidy, with unswept bedroom and kitchen floors and dirty clothes scattered around. One feels that Mrs Jones takes no pride in her home, and she fails to create a homely atmosphere.

Mrs O is deemed to have performed somewhat better than Mrs Jones in this regard:

The beds were made and the dining room floor was shining—even the back stoep [veranda] was swept and the bath as clean as possible under the circumstances. More often though the place was very much on the untidy side. It will encourage Mrs O a lot if we could have her back stoep painted red for her, and also if we could get her some coloured paper to paste on her bathroom window panes, which are at present simply smeared with some concoction passing by the name of brown paint. This looks very ugly and untidy.

To set the right example, social workers created a model cottage to illustrate the ideal way to furnish, organise and decorate your home. These ideals left lasting impressions.[10]

Throughout the 1940s, local housing associations had the ability to select their own residents. Potential candidates were thoroughly interviewed, and only the best candidates for upliftment were selected. In fact, in many cases race was less important than the aspiration to be a good white. During this era, behaviour was an important indication of colour. For example, a white person was defined as, 'in appearance obviously a white person or generally accepted as a white person.' A Coloured person who behaved and spoke like a white person and shared the cultural values and aspirations of a white person, could consequently be considered white. As a result of this subjective selection process, the first residents were well motivated, and with the support of the housing authorities they succeeded in uplifting themselves to the status of 'proper whites'.

In the 1950s things began to change. The election of the National Party to government in 1948 marked the start of apartheid proper. The regime incorporated the suburbs into its strategy of separate development for separate cultures, embodied by the Group Areas Act, and took over responsibility for selecting residents for the suburbs, leaving the local housing authorities without say. The definition of race, and hence place of residence, shifted from subjectively judged behavioural traits to a greater emphasis on racial biology. This created an interesting dilemma for the elite. So-called failed whites could no longer be reclassified as Coloured, yet their existence seriously undermined the case for white supremacy.[11]

By 1960, the economy was booming. As successful first residents moved out of these starter suburbs, purchasing homes in middle-class neighbourhoods, the government began to move in the 'failed whites' who lacked the capacity to join the middle class. While social engineering efforts and economic support for these people intensified, by the mid-sixties it had become clear that some white people simply could not be uplifted. Compassion turned to contempt and neighbourhoods such as Epping Garden Village began to be viewed as institutions for misfits rather than as communities. By 1980 the bulk of residents were single mothers, the elderly, the disabled, or alcoholics.

After the fall of apartheid, life in these suburbs changed drastically. State subsidies for the white residents were cancelled and social aid withdrawn. Unable to afford their cost of living, many residents dispersed to caravan parks or squatter camps. Socially aspiring Coloured people began moving in.

Today, Epping Garden Village is called Ruyterwacht. It is a working-class neighbourhood situated not far from Cape Town's high-end casino, GrandWest. The pine trees that used to line the streets in the 1940s are mostly gone, but the area still feels reasonably lush. The gardens outside the homely single-story houses continue to be well kept, as though the ghosts of social workers still wander these streets.

* * *

At the Senior Centre I meet 79-year-old Jean Faasen. Jean came here in 1960 with her husband and three children.

'There was nothing but a gravel road and bush around. But it was always very friendly,' she recalls.

GOOD WHITES, POOR WHITES

Jean used to work various jobs in factories and old-age homes, but when her first child was born her husband forced her to stay home to tend to the family. However, he didn't have a job, so every Friday social workers would come by with a box of food. In return, the family was subjected to strict rules and constant check-ups.

'They used to pop in whenever; at least twice a week,' she says.

They came to see if the children were alright, if the husband was making any progress in finding a job, and if the family was on the right path to becoming good whites.

'If someone had a drink on a Saturday night, come Monday morning there would be a letter in the mailbox saying: "If you can buy drinks, you can buy food," and you'd be kicked out,' Dumas, a friend of Jean's at the Senior Centre, recalls.

Jean still relies on welfare. At the centre she receives free coffee and, if she's lucky, a loaf of bread. Bread donations are distributed every week among the most needy community members.

In charge of bread distribution and kitchen duties is Shannon Parsons. She makes 200 rand a month, working three days a week. That is well below minimum wage and makes her the lowest-paid South African worker that I have met since my arrival in the country. Shannon is a middle-aged redhead, with fair skin; her face is covered in freckles. She has lived in the suburb for thirty years. She recalls how the town was not the best place to live when she moved in, and how it only got worse.

'Kind of depressing, really,' she says. 'Then they opened it up and Coloureds started buying the houses and fixing them up. It has made it a lot nicer here.'

Jean agrees. 'Now we have tarred roads and everything,' she says.

7

CASTAWAYS OF THE RAINBOW NATION

The neighbourhood of Kleingeluk (small happiness) in Orania is where the people Lottie refers to as 'them' live. These are the white people who, during apartheid, had to be either rehabilitated or hidden away, as their very existence disproved the fiction put forward by the Afrikaner elite; that the white race was genetically superior to the African. Kleingeluk is where the uneducated, the mentally disabled, the addicts, the felons, the failures, the has-beens and the never-weres of Orania live.

Tiny 'apartments', of less than ten sq m each, line the sides of a long single-storey building known as C-block. Originally built as stables, in the 1960s it housed black labourers from the Department of Water Affairs working on the irrigation scheme of nearby Vanderkloof dam. Meanwhile, the white population lived in airy bungalows on the other side of town, where the wealthier residents of Orania now reside.[1]

Nobody wants to let me in; perhaps they are ashamed of what I'll find. Besides, women aren't supposed to set foot in C-block. But finally Hugh Duranty, the caretaker, agrees to show me around. We walk through a tiny corridor where the walls look like they will collapse any second. All the doors are padlocked and Duranty claims he doesn't have the keys. On one door some-one has painted a swastika on the belly of a little smiling stick-man. The walls are made from mason blocks and there's no heating. This past winter temperatures fell as low as minus 13C.

'Ag, a couple of blankets and you're okay,' says Hugh. 'Besides, C-block is about to be renovated.'

Some Flemish and German donors have contributed funds to make living conditions here a little less deplorable.

Single men who have come to Orania to do manual labour are offered housing at C-block. At the time of my visit, in October 2011, there are thirty-five tenants. There is capacity to house a maximum of forty-two men, but at times it's far more crowded as some guys choose to share rooms, according to Hugh.

Hugh has been here just over a year. He used to be the man-ager of a farm, but when his fiancé passed away he came to Orania to 'see what it was all about'. He started helping on a farm before transitioning to garden work.

'At first I was embarrassed about it cause we're not used to seeing whites doing this type of labour ... working in the gardens ... women doing laundry. If someone came near when I was working I'd stop and start fiddling with my phone, pretending to be doing something different until they passed by,' he says.

After a while, a thin character with big, protruding ears approaches on a blue bicycle. His name is Riaan and he's a recent resident of C-block. He doesn't say much, but when I ask him, he proudly opens the door to his little shack. It is very neat, though the room contains nothing but an iron bed with a thin mattress. He motions for me to take a seat on his carefully made bed and then sits down beside me. He sits at the edge of the bed with a straight back and his hands neatly folded on his lap, like a young schoolboy eager to impress his teacher. I try to strike up a conversation, but Riaan only gives one-syllable answers to my questions, unable or unwilling to engage. He is missing most of his teeth and keeps his lips pressed tightly together, as though he is hoping that I won't notice. We sit in silence for a while, staring at his broken fan. Then I do my best to produce a heart-felt smile, thank him, and head back out into the corridor.

I round the corner and continue to D-block, a section of the former stables that houses bigger units intended for people who have been around for a while. Here I meet Peter. Peter is thirty-nine years old and has wild, constantly shifting, bright-blue eyes. He was raised as a missionary and talks a great deal about the Lord. Unlike Riaan, Peter chats incessantly and is very curious about the value systems of other countries. Besides moral values and the Lord, Peter has difficulties sticking to any one subject for more than fifteen seconds. He has been in Orania for four months. After two weeks he wanted to quit because the work was so hard, but he decided against it. He says he has no chance of finding work anywhere else so he sticks it out. Day by day he is growing to like it here. Most inspiring to him is the notion of self-sufficiency that Orania promotes. He thinks that it is less racist, and more respectful of his fellow man, than any other model he has known. He tries to explain this to the black truck drivers who pick him up as he hitchhikes to and from Orania. At first, he says, the truckers are suspicious and start with a very negative view of Orania. But he says he is often able to convince them of its merits.

I ask Peter to show me his room. Unlike Riaan, Peter is far from tidy. His room is bigger, but even less compelling than Riaan's. It contains a similar small iron bed, but with the addi-tion of a small camping stove. A piece of wood is attached to the wall, forming an improvised table. Everything is covered in filth, but Peter doesn't seem to care. He has invested in a small table fan and an old armchair with most of its stuffing falling out. A bookshelf built from cinderblocks houses his collection of books about farm murders and other South African atrocities. There is no water or sewage, no toilet or shower. The rent is 600 rand a month.

* * *

On their website, the Orania Movement explains how they want to 'provide a livelihood to marginalised Afrikaners.' C-block is referred to as the Elim Project, an effort to 'upgrade old single quarters for young men to occupy and provide labour for Orania.' According to the project's mission statement, 'Every effort is made to integrate these young men into the community, train them, and find work for them.' Men are 'selected on the basis of their support of the Afrikaner culture, religion and personal hygiene and neatness.'

A man in a bright-yellow T-shirt sits outside his room. Judging by the sign on his door, his name is A.P. le Roux. Le Roux saves most of his words for Polly, his little yellow canary who lives in a little yellow cage outside his room. I walk over to talk to him and to have a look at the bird. The door to his room is open and as I approach I can see that his bed is neatly made. Above it hangs a portrait of a sexy woman in underwear.

'I see that you have a little friend in there too,' I smile.

Horrified, Le Roux rushes over to the bed, rips the picture from the wall, and puts it face down on the bed. He's blushing. The others look at me with surprise.

'You're not angry?' someone asks.

'She has a sense of humour,' someone else remarks.

But Polly's owner, who appears to be in his fifties, won't look at me again. He stands staring at the ground, with blushing red cheeks.

'The biggest threat to South Africa right now is the Plague,' Peter comments.

'The Plague?' I ask.

'Yes. Pornography,' he says, his wild blue eyes open wide in a crazy stare. 'It corrupts people.'

The others nod in agreement. Even Dawid, who runs the little store in C-block and whom I soon come to know as someone with few moral boundaries, says he wouldn't dream of selling porn at his store.

'My Polish friend and I had an argument about whether South Africa should have a porn channel. Keep your porn to yourself I told him,' says Dawid.

8

VAGINA DENTATA

South Africa has one of the highest incidences of sexual violence in the world. One in four girls is likely to be raped before the age of sixteen, according to a 2002 report by the BBC. A common explanation is the myth that sexual intercourse with a virgin will cure a man of HIV.[1]

An alarming 28 per cent of South African men admit to having raped, according to a 2009 survey conducted by the Medical Research Council of South Africa (MRC). The MRC interviewed 1,738 South African men of all races and socio-economic backgrounds. The sample included rural as well as urban areas. Almost half who said they had raped admitted to having done so more than once.[2] According to the Cape Town-based organisation Rape Crisis, only one per cent of rapists are convicted.[3]

There are so many horror stories of rapes and assaults that some women prefer not to venture outside at all after dark. For those who still want to go out dancing and drinking on the weekend, Johannesburg has developed plenty of daytime party venues where the DJs stop playing at sunset. Here, the action starts as early as nine or ten in the morning and the crowd often consists mainly of white people who prefer not to leave their fortresses after dark. Caution rules. Some refuse to drink from open glasses, preferring bottles so they can keep their thumb over the opening. Some take even more drastic measures.

In 2005, Doctor Sonnet Ehlers invented an anti-rape device called Rape-aXe. It is reminiscent of a female condom but with small razor-sharp barbs embedded inside. The perpetrator does not feel it upon penetration, but when he starts to pull back, the little barbs drive into the skin of his penis causing excruciating pain.

'But there is hardly any blood, and if there is a drop or two it will stay inside the condom, minimising the risk for the transfer of disease,' says Ehlers.

Ehlers came up with the idea working as a blood technician at Kimberley Hospital in the late 1960s. There she met many rape victims and when one of them commented, 'If only I had teeth down there,' something clicked. Old folklore tales, likely conceived to discourage casual sex and rape, warn of the *vagina dentata* (Latin for toothed vagina). The thought of being able to turn the myth into a reality, inspired Ehlers, but back then the materials she needed just weren't available.

'When I told people I wanted plastic as sharp as fishhooks, they just laughed at me. But the word *can't* doesn't exist in my vocabulary,' says Ehlers.

By 2002 she finally found the right materials to use: a combination of plastics and polyurethane.

Over a period of eight years, between 2002 and 2010, Ehlers conducted research. She visited prisons across South Africa, speaking with rapists, trying to figure out what they look for in a victim and what would deter them. She also studied how women from different classes of South African society protect themselves from rape. Over the years she has seen some odd things, such as panties made from chains.

VAGINA DENTATA

'Some will insert sponges with embedded razors into their vaginas. But that can actually cause more damage to the woman than the man as it can pierce her uterus. There will also be lots of blood. One lady I met had super-glued razors to the lid of a can and inserted that into her vagina. Another common thing is to wear extremely tight bicycle shorts that are difficult for rapists to pull down. But girls wear them so tight it even makes it difficult for them to go to the toilet and it's very bad for blood circulation,' she tells me.

In rural areas Ehlers came across women wearing blankets around their waists. When she asked them why they would wear thick blankets in the heat, they allegedly replied that it was in order to have something to lie on when they were raped, as it was so uncomfortable on the bare ground.

Ehlers says that sometimes her mere presence in a village acted as a deterrent.

'I returned to one area three months after my first visit and they had not had a single rape since as the men were afraid I had left supplies behind for the women,' she says.

When I ask Ehlers why she thinks rape is so much more common in South Africa than in other countries around the world, she replies: 'Certain indigenous people can have as many wives as they want and can afford to support. Many men don't understand that they can't just take a woman because they feel like it; that it doesn't work like that. Even our president has multiple wives and was himself accused of rape not too long ago.'

9

SHOWER MAN

I first hear about President Jacob Zuma's sixth marriage on the radio. The reporter delivers the news with obvious sarcasm. Zuma is frequently portrayed as a silly old man of below average intelligence who struggles to keep it in his pants.

At the time of writing, Zuma has four wives. His third wife, Dr Nkosazana Dlamini-Zuma, divorced him in 1998, citing 'irreconcilable differences', and his second wife, Kate Mantsho, committed suicide in 2000. His twentieth child (by the ninth woman) became known to the world in 2010 and turned out to be the secret fruit of an extra-marital relationship with the daughter of an old family friend.

Many in the old guard of the ANC, not to mention the white community, thought Zuma unfit to represent their country. In their opinion, he embodied the almost clichéd caricature of the African leader, an uneducated polygamist heading into the election with only four years of schooling. And, to make matters worse, he was accused and tried on charges of both corruption and rape.

During his rape trial in 2006, Zuma claimed that the victim had insinuated that she wanted to have sex by wearing a *kanga* (a knee-length skirt); and that in Zulu culture it was the equivalent of rape to *not* have sex with a woman who was aroused. Zuma's supporters showed up at the trial shouting 'Burn the bitch, burn the bitch.'

Given that his accuser was a family friend whom Zuma knew to be HIV-positive, the prosecutor asked Zuma whether he had used protection. Zuma famously told the court that he had not worn a condom, but that he had quickly taken a shower afterwards to wash away the virus. This earned him the illustrious nickname the Shower Man. To this day he is still frequently portrayed by political cartoonist Jonathan Shapiro, aka Zapiro, with a shower above his head.

At the time of the trial, Zuma was deputy president and among his responsibilities was the overseeing of the country's HIV/Aids policy. In a country with some of the world's worst rape statistics and a high HIV infection rate exacerbated by rampant misinformation, this one example should be enough to disqualify a man from running for presidency. Instead, it had the opposite effect: his acquittal sparked wild celebrations.

Zuma is Zulu and his election as president in December 2007 therefore divided the ANC along tribal lines: Zulu party members voted for Zuma, while Xhosa party members largely voted for Mbeki.[1] Not only had race crept back into politics, but so had tribalism.

When the rape charges against Zuma were originally announced, many Zuma supporters suspected President Mbeki was behind them. The victim was an associate of Ronnie Kasrils, the KGB-trained Minister of Intelligence, and people speculated that Kasrils had recruited the lady as a honey-trap.

Zuma's sensationalist rape trial, with all its attendant outlandishness, seemed to occupy the minds of South Africans far more than the ongoing corruption charges he faced as the result of duplicitous arms deals.

In a push to modernise its defence equipment in 1999, South Africa had purchased a range of new arms equipment, including 28 JAS-39 Gripen fighter aircraft from Saab of Sweden and 24 Hawk aircraft from British Aerospace (BAe). The deal soon became subject to allegations of corruption.

In 2005, Zuma's financial advisor, Schabir Shaik, was sentenced to fifteen years in prison for having solicited bribes for Zuma. An investigation into Zuma's involvement in the deal was launched, causing Mbeki to fire Zuma as deputy president in 2005.[2]

Due to so-called procedural technicalities the case was dismissed, but not closed. On 28 December 2007, shortly after having been elected as President of the ANC, Zuma was served an indictment to stand trial in the High Court on various counts of racketeering, money laundering, corruption and fraud. Zuma appeared in court in August 2008, but in September the charges were declared unlawful on procedural grounds. Judge Chris Nicholson also stated that he believed political interference had played a role in the decision to recharge Zuma.[3]

In 2009, charges were reinstated on appeal, but again dropped as intercepted phone calls revealed that there had, in fact, been political conspiracy regarding the timing of the charges. The legal process was thereby 'tainted', but this was not to say that the charges had been ungrounded and the court made it clear the withdrawal of the charges was not to be confused with an acquittal.[4]

Every time Zuma appeared in court, the crowds outside grew larger. Supporters would *toyi-toyi* and sing 'Bring me my machine gun', the anti-apartheid song that swiftly became associated with Zuma. They told the world they were 'prepared to die for Zuma'[5] and informed the press that the Ten Commandments were an alien invention that didn't apply to African males.[6] They wanted a leader who was *of the people*; and, uneducated and with a poor background, Zuma appeared to be one of them. In May 2009, he was elected as president of South Africa.

But new evidence spurred yet another inquiry. In June 2011, Saab admitted that the alleged bribes had in fact been paid out by their former partner BAE Systems.[7] Auditors also claimed that German industrial company Ferrostaal had paid 300 million rand to secure the sale of submarines to South Africa.[8]

Later that year, President Jacob Zuma surprised the nation by appointing the Seriti Commission to investigate the 1999 arms deal once and for all.

In 2012, he was reelected as leader of the ANC.

By the end of September 2014, the cost of the Seriti Commission had risen to more than 80 million rand, 40 million of which had been used to pay the consultancy fees of a few well-connected individuals.[9] Meanwhile, the investigation itself had made little progress. The commission was accused of denying investigators access to key documents,[10] refusing important evidence, failing to call some important witnesses and censoring others. Several commissionaires resigned in protest.

In September 2014, more than thirty South African organisations, including Corruption Watch and Lawyers for Human Rights, demanded that the commission be dissolved and a proper criminal investigation launched.

Irrespective of the implications, on 7 May 2014, the South African public reelected Jacob Zuma to serve as their president until 2019.

16 DECEMBER 1938

'N VOLK HELP HOMSELF

'At the Blood River battleground you stand on sacred soil. It is here that the future of South Africa as a civilised Christian country and the continued existence of the responsible authority of the white race were decided ... You stand today in your own white laager at your own Blood River, seeing the dark masses gathering around your isolated white race.'

D.F. Malan, speech at the Day of the Vow commemorations, 1938

The year 1938 marked the centenary of the Battle of Blood River, and the commemorations were suitably epic. In a reenactment of the Great Trek, nine ox wagons retraced a symbolic journey from Cape Town to Pretoria. Afrikaners dressed in traditional Voortrekker clothing rushed out to greet the wagons as they passed through towns. Religious ceremonies were held, Afrikaner heroes celebrated, and streets renamed in their honour.

The journey took more than four months, culminating in Pretoria with the laying of the cornerstone of the Voortrekker Monument on 16 December.

In his speech at the centenary celebrations, D.F. Malan stirred the crowd with an impassioned call for Afrikaner self-reliance and willingness to fight for survival.[1] More than 100,000 people attended. The event was a turning point in Afrikaner unity and solidarity, spurring a revival of 16 December commemorations, solidifying the mythological past and strengthening Afrikaner nationalism.

The unifying celebrations of this era—and of 1938 in particular—are often cited as an important contributing factor to the coming to power of Malan's National Party (NP) in 1948. Another important factor was the resistance among Afrikaners to South Africa's participation in the Second World War.

On 4 September 1939, Prime Minister J.B.M. Hertzog, a general during the Second Anglo-Boer War, proposed to his cabinet that South Africa remain neutral in the Second World War. His subsequent motion to this effect in the House of Assembly was defeated by a vote of 80 to 67 that went largely along the lines of ethnic division in the white community: English-speakers versus Afrikaners. Hertzog then sought to dissolve Parliament and call a general election. The British Governor General refused his request and Hertzog was swiftly replaced by Jan Smuts. Smuts argued that intervention was necessary because 'the fate of humanity' and 'the future of our civilisation' was at stake. And although he had only half the cabinet on his side, Smuts took South Africa to war.[2]

Many Afrikaners resented having to fight alongside Britain, against Germany. Animosity towards the British was still widespread, and going to war on a split vote symbolised Britain's continued domination over the Afrikaners, causing many to question the very concept of democracy. Consequently, South Africa saw a growth in far-right activism.

The most important pro-Nazi, anti-war movement was the Ossewabrandwag (OB), a paramilitary organisation founded to perpetuate the spirit of the 1938 celebrations.[3] The OB rode the wave of Afrikaner disillusionment with democracy and managed to acquire as many as a 100,000 members. It rejected parliamentary politics and pinned its hopes on a German victory, which it hoped would lead to German assistance in establishing an Afrikaner republic. The OB also had an elite wing of storm-troopers, known as *Stormjaers*, who actively resisted the war through acts of sabotage and a handful of assassinations.[4]

In the early years of the war, it was still uncertain whether the National Party would also support the Nazis. But although Malan was firmly anti-war, the NP continued to support parliamentary politics and rejected National Socialism as well as violent resistance to the war. In 1941, members of the National Party were instructed to cut any ties with the Ossewabrandwag and open support for far-right organisations declined.[5]

However, support for the NP continued to grow, and in the 1943 election the party went from being a fairly insignificant force to being a feasible alternative and dangerous rival to the governing United Party (UP).[6]

* * *

The Dutch Reformed Church was the first body to formulate the doctrine of apartheid. The first printed record of the term dates back to a conference on missionary work in 1929. Reverend Jan Christoffel du Plessis argued that the Gospel had to be taught in a way that strengthened the African 'character, nature and nationality'. To ensure the survival of the Afrikaners and preserve the racial and cultural identity of black Africans, black and white had to worship separately. It was the Christian duty of white people to uplift the Africans 'on their own terrain, separate and apart'.[7]

Grateful for the opening the church had given them, National Party politicians and academics began to elaborate on the concept, turning apartheid into political ideology. They needed a way to exclude black people from the political system without relying on the principle of race alone. The biological basis of crude racist thinking had been discredited, and the idea that black or Coloured citizens should be repressed on account of their supposed racial inferiority was outdated. The buzzword in the 1930s segregation debate was 'cultural adaptation'. African cultures were depicted as different from, but not inferior to, those of the white populace and thus capable of developing along their own separate lines. This enabled leaders to make racist assumptions without being accused of basing them on an untenable theory of biological racism.[8]

Both the Afrikaners and the British were determined to preserve white dominance, but they disagreed over how best to do so. Afrikaners felt that the British lacked a sense of urgency, as securing dominance was not for them a matter of survival. If preserving their European blood proved too much of a challenge in Africa, the British could always capitulate and return home, Professor A.I. Malan, a nationalist MP, argued. And even if all of the British in Africa were to perish, their culture and heritage would not die out, as there would be millions of Englishmen left in Great Britain to carry on the British way of life. The Afrikaner, on the other hand, had no one outside of South Africa to carry his torch forward. For him, the question of survival had become 'an irresistible life force, a veritable obsession'. The Afrikaner language, history, traditions, calling and culture had all originated in South Africa and there was a strong sense of belonging attached to the soil.[9]

Minister of Finance Nicolaas Havenga said: 'As far as the Afrikaners are concerned we cannot get out. We dare not adopt a policy that would make it possible for us to be driven out, because we—the Afrikaners—have no other home in which we can take refuge.'[10]

In 1943, the idea of apartheid was cementing; the National Party's mouthpiece, *Die Burger*, in that year referred to 'the accepted Afrikaner viewpoint of apartheid.' In 1944, Malan first used the term in Parliament; he said: 'I do not use the term "segregation", because it has been interpreted as a fencing off [afhok], but rather "apartheid", which will give the various races the opportunity of uplifting themselves on the basis of what is their own.'[11]

Apartheid was a philosophy based on paternalism and trustee-ship. White citizens had to help inferior people to climb the ladder of civilisation so that they might develop according to the natural aptitudes and capacities of their race. Only then could white and Coloured communities coexist alongside each other in 'friendship and cooperation'.[12]

In 1945, the National Party adopted apartheid as its official racial policy.[13] But pro-apartheid sentiments filtered into the United Party as well. While Jan Smuts and his government moved towards the economic integration of non-whites to satisfy the increased demand for labour in the booming war economy, they simultaneously increased residential segregation. In 1941, employers were required by law to segregate work, recreation and eating areas, and new suburbs were built specifically for non-white people. Even beaches were segregated.[14]

In Durban, many South Africans of Asian descent—the major-ity Indian—had managed to acquire a great deal of property in the so-called white town. Although they made up only three per cent of the population, they owned nineteen per cent of all retail enter-prises in the country. As a result, the Smuts government froze all property transactions between white and Asian South Africans. In 1946, 'white areas' and 'Asian areas' were created as separate from one another, and Asian residents were no longer allowed to buy property in designated 'white' areas.[15]

Franchise was largely restricted to the white population. Only in the Cape Province had non-whites ever been entitled to vote, but over the years more and more restrictions had been put in place. In 1930 the franchise was extended to white women, but not to black or Coloured women. A year later the literacy and property requirements were repealed for white voters but not for black or Coloured voters. In 1936, black men were removed altogether from the common voters' roll in the Cape. As compensation they were allowed to elect three white representatives to the House of Assembly, four senators, and a Natives Representative Council with advisory powers only. As a result, South Africa's white minority had virtually complete political control.

When the 1948 election campaign began, the United Party was in trouble. Afrikaners had been seriously alienated from the party by the decision to enter the Second World War and what they perceived as discrimination against Afrikaners during the conflict. Meanwhile, not only had the wages of white workers fallen, but large numbers of black workers had also entered the labour market. This, along with industrialisation, frightened white workers, especially the unskilled. Between 1945 and 1948, the number of unemployed white males nearly doubled, increasing from 76,000 to 139,000. Then, the UP government announced a plan to import 50,000 immigrants each year to alleviate the shortage of skilled labour.[16]

Farmers were struggling to make ends meet as the prices of supplies and equipment rose faster than those of produce. There was also a crisis in labour relationships, with farmers complaining that Africans 'had lost respect for them' and that a 'strained relationship had come to replace the old forms of coexistence'. During the war, the Smuts government had relaxed the influx control that kept rural black residents on the farms. Consequently, many farm workers had left for the cities where salaries were much higher. The government ignored pleas for intervention, but the NP promised to do better by intensifying control over African farm workers through the institution of pass laws that would prevent them from leaving at will.[17]

It was the farmers who decided the outcome of the 1948 election. In spite of winning only forty per cent of the popular vote, the NP—in alliance with the Afrikaner Party, with whom they merged in 1951—won a majority of five seats.[18] D.F. Malan became prime minister pledging to uplift the Afrikaner and free him from British subjugation. He also promised a final solution to the 'native question' or 'black peril' that threatened the long-term survival of the Afrikaner. That final solution was apartheid.[19]

10

BLOOD BROTHERS

'The South African Government today is the Broederbond and the Broederbond is the Government. No Afrikaner government can rule South Africa without the support of the Broederbond. No Nationalist Afrikaner can become Prime Minister unless he comes from the organisation's select ranks.'

Ivor Wilkins and Hans Strydom, *The Super-Afrikaners*

The rise of the National Party and apartheid ideology would not have been possible were it not for a secret brotherhood known as Die Afrikaner Broederbond. By making sure the most influential Afrikaners in South Africa were on its list of members, it worked to advance the cause of Afrikaners in any way it could.

It all started on 18 April 1918, with the meeting of three young Afrikaners in Kensington, Johannesburg. They decided to form a society that would 'defend the Afrikaner and return him to his rightful place in South Africa'.[1] Their organisation would soon rise to become one of the most influential secret societies in the world.

The Second Anglo-Boer War had left the Afrikaners poor, traumatised and without political influence. Since their farmlands had been destroyed through the British Empire's scorched-earth policy, large numbers of Afrikaners were forced to migrate to the cities where they struggled to make a living.

The Broederbond set out to help Afrikaners adapt and make a successful transition to urban life while remaining Afrikaners. Great effort was placed on furthering the Afrikaans language, preventing the establishment of an integrated Afrikaans–English culture and promoting a Christian ethos. The two main pillars of Afrikaner Christian Nationalism were the portrayal of Afrikaners as a chosen people and of racial segregation as God's will.[2] The Broederbond also played an important role in rescuing the Afrikaner from poverty, in educating the people and in the 'rehabilitation' of poor whites. The organisation started—or helped start—social and economic upliftment schemes, as well as banks, media empires, industries, financial institutions and universities. Membership was by exclusive invitation only and to be eligible you had to be a Protestant Afrikaner man with a spotless reputation.

With the election victory of the National Party and the implementation of apartheid, the Broederbond amassed great power, penetrating every aspect of Afrikaner life. Its members were everywhere that mattered. They were found in town and city councils, school and company boards, agricultural unions, media outlets, industry, commerce and banks.[3]

At its peak the Broederbond consisted of between 12,000 and 18,000 prominent Afrikaners from all sectors of society. By the 1970s, successful companies owned by Afrikaners made up the bulk of the South African economy. The civil service was run and staffed mostly by Afrikaners and the South African Railways was used to provide employment to unskilled and uneducated Afrikaners.

Whether the Broederbond as an organisation governed South Africa is debatable, but that it was Broeders who for many years ruled the country is beyond doubt. All prime ministers and state presidents between 1948 and 1990 were Broeders; only a few cabinet ministers during this period were not members.

The organisation was inarguably an important one, and they knew it. Members were believed to be on a divine mission, or as Dr Meyer, chairman of the Broederbond between 1960 and 1972, put it: 'Broerskap—the Afrikaner Broederbond—is a gift from God to our *volk* ... to strive and realise its separate destiny to the greater glory of His name.'[4]

With increased power came delusions of grandeur, and what started out as an organisation for economic upliftment soon took an insidious turn. In 1968, at the fiftieth anniversary of the Broederbond, Henning Klopper, one of the founding members and first chairman said:

> Do you realise what a powerful force is gathered here tonight between these four walls? Show me a greater power on the whole continent of Africa! Show me a greater power anywhere, even in your so-called civilised countries!
>
> We are part of the State, we are part of the Church, we are part of every big movement that has been born of the nation. And we make our contributions unseen; we carried them through to the point that our nation has reached today.[5]

The importance the Broeders placed on themselves and in their organisation was extreme. When someone dared ask whether the time had not come for the Broederbond to dissolve, as it had clearly achieved its purpose, Klopper replied: 'If that is so, Broeders, then we must ask: who will give us the Government of the country? Who will give us our future Prime Ministers? Who is to mould them? Where are they to come from? Where will they be found? [...] What would have happened to the Afrikaner *volk* if the Broederbond had ceased to exist? Our nation depends on the Broederbond.'[6]

11

JACK OF ALL TRADES

'When I first came to Orania I thought: What the hell is this? Not even a black man would stay here, never mind a white,' says Dawid.

Dawid is in his mid-fifties but still has the eyes and bowl cut of a mischievous boy. He is extremely thin; every part of his body seems to be slipping away from him. What little shoulder bone he has slopes forward to the point where there is not much left to hang his shirt on. Even his cheeks, pulling away from his eyes, leave his skin hanging from his face. He is an avid smoker and while he looks rather unhealthy, is full of energy. On the rare occasions he does stop, he leans against a wall and puts his hands in his pockets to keep them still.

Dawid has been in Orania for two years. He misses the sophistications of the big city. He's into ballroom and Latin American dancing, neither of which can be found in Orania; nor can his son or relatives, who live in Cape Town. But on the other hand, he says there is good money to be made here, and more peace of mind.

About a year after arriving, he started a shop, which he runs concession-style out of C-block, selling merchandise over an improvised counter. Sweets, crackers and canned foods are neatly stacked on the shelves, filling every inch of space. He imports most of his merchandise from a Turkish warehouse in Johannesburg and sells it so cheaply that it has gotten him in trouble with the other local shopkeepers, who claim his prices are so low they are unable to compete. After his first few months in business he was forced to close down, but he fought his way back.

'I petitioned and got my shop back,' he says proudly. 'I'm the first person in Orania to ever petition an eviction.'

Dawid's store generates between 50,000 and 60,000 rand in income each month. As we talk we're often interrupted by workers stopping to buy chocolates or cigarettes. Dawid says he sells around two thousand packs of cigarettes each month. That would mean an average of just under seventy packs a day, which, given the steady stream of customers during my visit, does not seem unlikely. He pulls out a box of Grand-Pa headache powder; it's another one of his bestsellers and he claims to average 76 packs every night.

'Sometimes the same guy will pick up 10 or 20 packs a night. Some even smoke the powder,' says Dawid.

Many of the guys at C-block have a history of alcohol and drug abuse, and since neither drugs nor drinking are allowed, painkillers seem to take their place—painkillers, tobacco and sugar.

The store is only open in the evening as everybody is at work during the day, including Dawid, although he doesn't really need the other jobs anymore.

'I help a guy who has a little coin shop. I do a bit of everything: I look after his kids and even do some cleaning or cooking. And then I do some work in gemstones.'

Dawid is looking for a facility where he can open his own cutting works. It's a little tricky as he needs something secure, he says; something with concrete floors. Still, it would be way easier here than in South Africa, which Dawid speaks about as though it were a separate country.

'In South Africa I would need a black economic partner who would get fifty per cent of my profits. Then I would also have to pay tax. Here they can't force me to have a black partner and so they can't force me to register at all. Besides, no one comes here to check the documents.'

He says he buys his precious stones—mainly tanzanite—from Tanzania.

'Then I sell them on without documentation or nothing,' he tells me. 'Sometimes I cut and polish them myself; sometimes I just sell them the way they are. I deal with diamonds as well. I've been trading openly for years. I'd rather give fifty per cent of the profit to the cause of this place than to some black guy I don't even know and who doesn't even work.'

Dawid says he buys most of his diamonds from Zimbabweans.

'I know it's illegal, but I don't feel guilty about that. I'm helping to support a lot of families. I'm sure you've heard about "blood" diamonds. Anything that Europeans value, like copper, gas or oil, you must put "blood" in front of. Black people don't care about that stuff. They can't eat it. Black people value power and land. Only a drop of the profits gets back to the blacks anyway.'

As the mover and shaker of C-block, Dawid has a fancier place than most, one with its own shower and toilet. But he likes to stay close to the rest of the guys to 'keep an eye on things'.

'We especially keep a close watch on newcomers. It's not just blacks who commit crimes. Half these guys come from prison; they're either ex-cons, straight out of rehab or from the streets. They come here for a second chance,' says Dawid.

He walks me over to his place. It's neat and organised, just like his shop. One of his tables is covered with little jars of jam made from different local berries. I ask him about them.

'Oh those ... well you know there are all these berries here that nobody is using, so I figured somebody ought to do something with that.'

So Dawid gathered ten of Orania's unemployed women and put them to work making jam. He bought all the necessary supplies and now pays them five rand per jar for the labour.

He is the ultimate entrepreneur and opportunist: retailing, distributing, importing and exporting, even producing, anything from precious stones, ivory and animal skins, to chocolate and jam.

Dawid's little shop doubles as a pawnshop. At one point, Dawid extended credit, but he says a lot of drifters come through Orania so he has stopped that. These days, those who don't have the money, barter. One evening he sold off twelve old cellphones that people had used as currency.

'Anything people want to sell I'll buy, mark it up a little, and pass on,' he tells me.

In every corner, drawer, or stashed away box in his tiny shop, there is some seemingly random object waiting to be sold.

'I also have lots of Chinese stuff here,' Dawid says, pointing to a section of the shop where cheap wallets and all sorts of trinkets line the shelves.

Then he pulls out a newspaper with an article about a restaurant in China that supposedly specialises in serving the foetuses of aborted human babies. The story is an obvious hoax and I'm not sure if Dawid believes it himself or if he just enjoys shocking people. Either way, the photos of foetuses on dinner plates are very disturbing and so Dawid shows them to anyone who has any moral reservations about his 'blood diamonds' or other businesses.

'If you want to consider the morality of something, consider this,' he says and slams the pictures down on the counter of his store. 'The Chinese are so damn powerful nobody will touch them.'

In Dawid's mind, people who think Oranians are racists are totally misguided. Orania is nothing compared to what he calls 'South Africa'. He speaks of his friends in Matsap; a rural area about 300 km north-west of Orania, where he claims nothing has changed since the end of apartheid.

'They'll pay their black workers 45 rand a month and give them food rations. And blacks are told never to speak to a white man unless spoken to first and never to make eye contact. Even when they come to collect their food, they will stand there in the dirt and the white guy will not hand over the food, but drop it in the dirt in front of their feet so they must bend down to pick it up.'

That's too much, even for Dawid. 'It's one thing to be proud of your culture, but you should still be human about it,' he says.

When we're alone in the shop, Dawid tells me about 'Uhuru' or 'Night of the Long Knives', a prediction by the late Boer prophet Nicolaas 'Siener' van Rensburg, frequently recited by Afrikaners all over the country.

'They are waiting for a sign to rise up and kill all white people. War will break out in Europe, but the Germans will come and help us. This time we will drive them all the way back to the Zambezi. It will be genocide. Both sides will attempt to kill everybody, including women and children. But make no mistake, people are prepared. This has been planned for many years. There are sixty-four radical groups all over the country and they are very organised,' Dawid says.

According to Dawid, Orania is just a distraction from where the real war preparations are going on.

'There's nothing here. No weapons. We're just a diversion.'

He too is prepared to fight.

'It has nothing to do with hating black people. It's about preserving our own,' he says.

I find myself spending more and more time at Dawid's shop. It's the evening hub for C-block residents, the one place that is always busy in the otherwise eerily quiet town, and hence the best place to meet people.

One night, as we're talking, a customer arrives and asks for two packs of Shasha, a cigarette brand I've never seen before.

Dawid notices my inquisitive look as he hands over the packs and quickly explains: 'These cigarettes are illegal because the manufacturers don't pay tax. They are from Botswana and are being sold at 12 rand a pack.'

A regular pack of cigarettes is around thirty rand. No wonder Dawid's merchandise is walking off the shelves.

But every now and then Dawid's sketchy business gets him into trouble. He tells me how some time ago he was caught with a big box of illegal cigarettes in his car.

'If they catch you, you get huge fines and can even go to jail. But they just asked me, "What can you do for us so that we don't have to open this box?" I gave them a thousand rand and they just said: "Get out of here,"' he says.

As we talk, the shop gets busier. I've forgotten that, as a woman, I'm not really supposed to be here and it's obvious that the men aren't used to it. Many of them are dirty after a hard day working the soil. They look at me like prisoners who haven't seen a woman in years.

Peter, who showed me his unit at D-block, comes by. He is bare-chested; his wild blue eyes are wide open. He starts talking about the Vikings and the Viking traditions.

'Are you pagan?' he asks.

'What about Sweden, what is life like there?'

'How would one court a Swedish lady?'

'Are Swedish ladies attracted to black men?'

Peter shoots one question after the other, hardly giving me time to respond and standing so close it makes me feel uncomfortable.

I tell him the obvious: that it varies from woman to woman.

'But what about a black man would they find attractive? Is it that it is something exotic?' Peter persists. 'Because to us it is just inconceivable.'

The other men all nod, agitated now. They've formed a tight circle around me and are watching my face intently, waiting for an answer, an explanation, waiting for something I can't deliver.

'But there are plenty of mixed-race people in South Africa, so it obviously happens,' I object.

'The browns were fine when we were making them, but not when they started making themselves,' says Dawid and starts laughing, revealing a few gaps from missing teeth. The others chuckle.

'It's a joke!' he says, as I remain serious. 'It's just a joke!'

While his comment is crude, it serves to break the tension that has been building in the circle around me. The men laugh so hard their chests heave, and I take my chance to slip away and leave the store.

12

AN INCONVENIENT YOUTH

It is 27 October 2011 and the mood of white Johannesburg is thick with fear and foreboding. Elaborate barbed wired fences line the sidewalks leading towards the Johannesburg Stock Exchange (JSE). A few white-collar workers have taken cover behind the security barricades, waiting for signs of the destructive mob that is anticipated at any moment.

It is the first day of the ANC Youth League's two-day march for economic freedom. The demonstrators have already delivered a memorandum at the Chamber of Mines in downtown Johannesburg, demanding nationalisation of the mines. Now they are on their way to the JSE to protest their lack of economic opportunities. From here, it's on to Pretoria where President Zuma will be confronted about his plans to tackle unemployment.

A few weeks previous, on 30 August, there were violent clashes between ANC Youth League supporters and police officers in Johannesburg's city centre. Supporters of Julius Malema, the Youth League President, started fires, burning ANC flags, and posters depicting President Zuma's face. They also managed to break off chunks of the concrete barricades, hurling glass bottles and stones at police officers and journalists. When they threatened to breach the barbed wire surrounding the ANC's headquarters at Luthuli House, police responded by firing rubber bullets and teargas in an effort to contain the chaos.[1/2]

Today, people have been warned to stay clear and police reinforcements stand ready. Maps outlining roads to avoid have appeared in the newspapers. Many companies have tightened their security and let their employees off early. As a temporary resident of the area, I've had several maps and timetables slipped under my door. The management of the apartment building where I live is adamant about keeping us indoors.

* * *

The gap between South Africa's haves and have-nots is among the highest in the world and growing by the day. The country's unemployment statistics are depressing. In 2011, 50 per cent of all 15–24 year olds were unemployed, according to the Institute of Race Relations (IRR).[2] Many of them are poor, angry and desperate for someone to represent them. In their eyes Julius Malema personifies this long-awaited leader.

Malema speaks directly to the masses, addressing issues that he argues the ANC has failed to deal with: issues of poverty, unemployment and race. That he has himself become a millionaire by using his political connections to access government tenders seems not to bother his supporters—and Malema does little to hide it. He drives top of the range cars, owns several expensive properties, throws lavish parties and is known for his $34,000 Breitling watch. He claims many of his possessions come from generous 'comrades'.[3]

'We are the elite that has been deliberately produced by the ANC as part of its policy to close the gap between whites and blacks in this country,' he told the *Sowetan* in 2008.[4]

Born in 1981 and raised in poverty in the Limpopo town of Seshego, Malema is the only son of a domestic worker. He joined the ANC at the age of nine when he was allegedly recruited to a secret militant unit. He quickly climbed the political ranks and at fourteen he was the leader of the ANC youth branch in his town. Having nothing else to cling to, politics became his life and he soon formed powerful alliances deep within the party. In 2007, he was active in the behind-the-scenes battle that forced Mbeki to resign as president, and put Jacob Zuma in his place.

When Zuma was facing rape charges, Malema famously stated that he would kill for him. He also suggested that the woman accusing Zuma of rape had a 'nice time,' a statement that later earned him a conviction for hate speech.

In 2008, Malema was elected leader of the ANC Youth League, and he hasn't left the limelight since. The ultimate populist, he uses every available opportunity to grab headlines with his communist politics and racist remarks. Among many white South Africans his mere existence causes so much anxiety that it has given rise to a phenomenon known as Malemaphobia.

One of Malema's most infamous ploys was his resurrection of the old struggle song *Dubula iBhunu*, 'Shoot the Boer', which he first performed in March 2010, at a rally at the University of Johannesburg's Doornfontein campus.

White Africa erupted. A multitude of lawsuits, investigations and formal complaints were lodged against Malema by those claiming the song would spark racial hatred and violence.

On 26 March 2010, the South Gauteng High Court in Johannesburg ruled that the song was 'unconstitutional and unlawful.'[5] The ANC appealed the ruling and the case was referred to the Equality Court. In the meantime, the party declared that Malema must refrain from singing *Dubula iBhunu* in public. But Malema ignored the order and continued to perform it.

On 3 April 2010, Eugene Terre'Blanche, leader of the ultra-right minority party The Afrikaner Weerstandsbeweging (AWB), was beaten to death by two of his farm workers. In spite of a complete absence of ties between the perpetrators and the Youth League leader, the media still pointed their fingers at Malema.

A year later, Malema was charged with hate speech for continuing to sing 'Shoot the Boer'. His trial was broadcast on national television. Although he was eventually convicted, and banned from singing the song, many argue that the courtroom drama actually increased his popularity. In defending his singing of 'Shoot the Boer' and other struggle songs, Malema became a hero in the eyes of many poor black South Africans. The ANC lined up behind him and so Malema began to push the boundaries even further.

In a campaign for local elections in May 2011, he referred to white people as 'criminals' who 'must be treated as such' and urged his supporters to 'take the land without paying.'[6] The crowd, gathered at the Galeshewe Stadium in Kimberley, cheered. President Zuma, who was right next to him on stage, did not object to Malema's rhetoric.

A few weeks later, in June 2011, Malema was re-elected as leader of the Youth League. He was unopposed.

* * *

I reach the JSE well ahead of the protest. Two-metre high barricades of concrete and razor wire line the road, separating the protesters' route, where I stand, from the sidewalks and buildings. The riot police position themselves at the front, well armed behind large shields and helmets. Behind it all, local television journalists are busy rigging their cameras.

Two Afrikaners who work at a nearby Nedbank approach and ask if I'm a journalist.

'You're obviously not South African,' one of them remarks.

I explain that I have come to observe and photograph the march. They offer to let me up to the balcony of the bank and watch the march from there, like they intend to themselves.

'No thanks,' I reply. 'I'll get better photos from down here.'

'Don't you value your life? Look around, there's a reason there is no other white person here.'

'I'll be fine,' I say.

After a few more attempts at convincing me, they shake their heads in resignation, turn around, and walk away. Then, about ten metres down the road, one of them turns back.

'If you die, can I have your camera?' he asks.

Although I think they are silly, I'm relieved when another journalist joins me on the 'wrong' side of the barricades. His name is Willem and he works as a freelancer in the Mozambican capital city of Maputo. Today, however, he is on temporary assignment to cover the Youth League demonstration.

We make a few predictable, but unavoidable comments about being the minority and the underlying stress that this can entail.

'I'm relieved and surprised when a black person is nice to me,' says Willem. 'Because really they should hate me; they should hate us after everything we've done.'

Even though he was born and raised just outside of Johannesburg, Willem felt he had to move to Maputo to get to know the *real* Africa. In South Africa he felt unable to break the segregation as the lives of black and white people still run parallel to one another.

'Maybe at university there was a chance to make a black friend or two, but that's really it. It wasn't until I moved to Maputo that I became used to being surrounded by blacks all the time,' he tells me.

He takes out his phone and shows me an email, one of the many absurd chain letters circulating in South Africa. This one claims that today will be 'The Red Day' and cautions Afrikaners to stay away during the Economic Freedom March as, according to the letter, Malema has announced that on 27, 28 and 29 October, he and his crew will be out to rape white women. The letter is in

Afrikaans so Willem gives me a brief translation. I laugh, but it rings hollow. When everyone around you is afraid it is difficult to remain unaffected. With growing anxiety, we wait.

* * *

We hear the drums first. A distant, rhythmic menace. Then, the sound of thousands of feet, thundering as one. A symphony of anger. Closer. Louder. Now voices: shouting; chanting. And then they appear.

The first wave is small. A hundred people or so. Up and down they dance, arms in the air. They carry signs stating their demands and assuring supporters of certain victory. I stand to the side, close to the razor wire, to let them pass. A group on my side of the road notices me. I tense up, but their eyes pass me by as if I were nothing more than a lamppost. Their anger is not directed at me. On they go. Dancing. Chanting.

Like a long parade, the first group goes out a bit ahead of the main group and I stare at the empty road behind them. But the noise from the next wave pours into the space. Louder and louder. And then it hits. This time there are thousands. I have heard of the *toyi-toyi*, the war dance of the townships, but never seen it; and I have certainly never been consumed by it as I am now. The marchers are running on the spot, jumping up and down and chanting with a seemingly boundless anger. I know they have already been running for seven hours. They will keep this same pace for two days. It reminds me of footage I have seen in videos at the Apartheid Museum from the great ANC mass protests towards the end of apartheid. Only this time the riot police are black and the white people are bystanders, some paralysed with fear, others arrested by the sheer momentum of it all.

I press myself further to the side, leaning into the barbed wire now. The mob rushes past me, like a raging river impatient to arrive at the cliff where it will explode into the roaring froth of a waterfall. The noise is all-consuming; the pace constantly increasing, without ever missing a beat. I take a few steps towards the stream of demonstrators, as if to test the current. I am standing at the edge of the pavement, hesitating, when I am overcome by the sensation of being watched. I look up to find that the white bankers and stock exchange brokers on the balconies all have their eyes glued to my blond head in the crowd. But, judging by their faces, their attention does not stem from concern. Like the spectators at a public execution, they are waiting for blood, for retaliation, maybe even for justice. But most of all they are waiting for confirmation of the black violence they have been bred to fear.

I step out into the stream of demonstrators. Their pace is fast; I have to jog just to keep up. Suddenly, a huge man wearing the black beret of the ANC Youth League makes a mock charge towards me. He is covered in chains; heavy leg irons clanging from his neck, knotted at his chest. His face is contorted with rage. He comes close enough to terrify me, turning only at the last moment when he has achieved his objective. Most, however, simply ignore my presence. Old and young, women and men, all are caught up in the dance and chant. Faces covered with sweat, they move together as though in a trance. They don't walk, march, or even demonstrate; they float.

Next to me a middle-aged woman is dancing, but even though we bump into each other she does not appear to notice me. Her face is turned upwards towards the sky and her gaze is distant. Some teenage boys have crafted mock machine guns from wood and cardboard. They appear to be aiming them at the men on their balconies, and scream 'rat-a-tat-tat'. In clear red script, their signs demand ECONOMIC FREEDOM IN OUR LIFETIME or declare ONLY JULIUS MALEMA CAN SAVE US! While many are dressed in regular jeans and T-shirts, there are also plenty of supporters wearing berets, shirts and, strung around their necks, placards hailing the slain Colonel Gaddafi as an anti-imperialist martyr.

Following the death of Gaddafi, I was surprised to come across several editorials paying tribute to the Libyan dictator. In some South African media, Gaddafi was portrayed as a leader who raised his country's literacy rate from twenty-five to eighty per cent; who provided guaranteed housing schemes, interest-free loans and free electricity. In Europe, the media cried 'good riddance' at the news of his death, celebrating a world with one less tyrant. The only debate centered on the morality of his execution and the public display of his corpse. Few questioned the underlying notion that this was an evil man who needed to be removed from power. And I certainly didn't hear of any fans hawking Gaddafi-emblazoned T-shirts or throwing parties in his honour.

A man wearing a black Gaddafi shirt climbs halfway up the fence, waving his fist at the crowd. Behind him is Exchange Square, its predominantly white bankers lined up safely behind the fence. I photograph the freedom fighter against this back-drop, then I too climb the fence to get some overview shots of the crowd. As I do, three young men notice me. They scream something I can't understand, but judging by the face of an older protester beside them, it's not pretty. His face contracts in dis-gust and disbelief and, as the youngsters turn and begin to head in my direction, he takes one of them by the arm and shakes him, as if scolding a disobedient child. The others give me one last wave of their fists before turning to follow their friend.

A little shaken, I climb back down from the fence to merge once again with the stream of people.

13

SHOOT THE BOER

On 10 November 2011, Malema is found guilty of provoking divisions within the ANC and of bringing it into disrepute. After a long process of appeals he is eventually expelled from the party and forced to surrender his leadership of the ANC Youth League. Still, few Afrikaners have any illusions that he is politically dead.

'He's like Arnold Schwarzenegger in *Terminator 2*,' says Alana Bailey. '*I'll be back ...*'

Alana Bailey and Ernst Roets are the deputy chief executives of AfriForum, the Afrikaner civil rights group that took Malema to court for singing 'Shoot the Boer.' I meet them in their Pretoria office where posters of a gagged Malema line the walls. In the poster, Malema has a stop sign pasted over his mouth. The headline reads STOP MALEMA! The poster goes on to describe, in Afrikaans, what people can to do help.

'There is a lot of racial hatred,' Roets tells me. 'There is a climate being created where it is okay to hate white people; it's okay to sing that white people are dogs and should be shot.'

Roets believes that this atmosphere of racial hatred whipped up by the likes of Malema legitimises violence against the Boers and hence contributes to the increasing rate of murder of white farmers.

In March 2010, after launching the hate speech complaint against Malema—but prior to the court case—AfriForum planned a protest march to the ANC's headquarters. They wanted to present Malema with a memorandum explaining why they wanted him to stop singing 'Shoot the Boer'. The memorandum contained the names of 1,600 victims of farm attacks. But in order to carry out the protest march they needed a letter from Malema saying that he would accept the memorandum, so Roets went to meet with him.

'Malema said he would only sign the letter if AfriForum dropped the case against him. So we asked him if he would stop singing the song. Malema replied: "We will never stop singing that song",' Roets continues.

'We debated language issues and affirmative action. Finally we told him that we would carry out the protest march regardless of whether he was willing to accept the memorandum or not. Then he told us that if we did, what happened to the protestors at the IFP march in 1994 would happen to us,' says Roets.

On 28 March 1994, supporters of the Inkatha Freedom Party (IFP) marched to the ANC headquarters in Johannesburg in protest of the upcoming elections. ANC security guards opened fire, killing 19.

When later questioned about this in court, Malema admitted that he had advised against the march, but denied having threatened anyone. However, the ANC refused to release their audio recording of the meeting and it remained a case of word against word.

Too frightened to carry out the march after the meeting with Malema, AfriForum protesters gathered the following day on Mary Fitzgerald Square, about three streets away from the ANC headquarters at Luthuli House. A small delegation, consisting of

Roets and four others, then continued on alone to Luthuli House to drop off the memorandum at the reception. The police were waiting for them, and they blocked the delegation from entering. AfriForum's Kallie Kriel acted quickly; he threw the memorandum over the heads of the police and through the open door, where it landed at the feet of some ANC members. The party members, assisted by some of the police officers, picked up the document and proceeded to crumple up the pages and throw them out onto the pavement. There, the pages, printed with the names of the deceased, were trodden on and kicked into the gutter. This caused an outcry among many Afrikaners, who felt it disrespectful of the victims. Photos of the crumpled sheets of paper appeared across local newspapers the following day.

On 12 September 2011, Malema was found guilty of hate speech in the Gauteng High Court.

'The ANC made the Malema case a party issue. In the hate speech trial, we went after him, not the party; but the party lined up behind him, saying that he was not a loose cannon,' says Roets. 'When Malema got kicked out of the ANC, it was for criticising Jacob Zuma, not for inciting racial hatred. They stood by him on that.'

Roets believes there is a problem with the ideological DNA of the ANC.

'Malema is a product of the ANC. The ANC Youth today couldn't be more unlike the ANC Youth fifty years ago,' he says, and goes on to explain how the white population has become a punching bag for politicians trying to garner support.

'Black unemployment is through the roof. The government hasn't delivered on its promises. They can't blame themselves so they continue to blame apartheid, saying that it was so bad they still can't deliver. They need a scapegoat,' he argues.

Roets and Bailey claim racial tensions are currently the highest they've been since the end of apartheid.

'We have to constantly monitor our Facebook page and remove racist comments. Malema supporters will write things like "We'll kill you" and the Afrikaners will reply, "We'll kill you first." It's the worst it's been since 1994,' says Bailey.

But at the same time, growing racial tensions serve organisations like AfriForum well. Membership has soared in recent times. Founded in 2005, by 2010 the organisation had 10,000 members. By December 2011, that number had more than tripled, reaching 32,000 members. What started with three employees now had thirty.[1]

In 2011, the organisation began encouraging the establishment of local branches. Less than a year later there were thirty-seven branches, all of them staffed by volunteers.

AfriForum deals mainly with issues relating to civic rights, environment, crime and heritage. For example, in the town of Winburg municipal refuse is being dumped into a churchyard. AfriForum has warned the municipality to resolve the matter or they will take legal action.

After the murder of Eugene Terre'Blanche in April 2010, chain letters issuing warnings of impending atrocities began to circulate around the Afrikaans community. A common topic was the so-called Night of the Long Knives, which Dawid in Orania first told me about, but which I would soon hear repeated by many others. With the appearance of each letter, AfriForum is buried in emails and phone calls from terrified Afrikaners. The organisation then carries out extensive research, contacting legal and security experts at the universities to get their assessment.

'We have to take each one seriously because otherwise it becomes like crying wolf. If a real threat does appear, no one will listen,' says Bailey.

AfriForum also does its best to trace the origin of the letters, even going so far as to issue a reward for the source of the rumours. But, as the letters are frequently traced to false

Facebook accounts, finding and prosecuting those responsible is near impossible.

* * *

In 2013, Julius Malema formed his own political party, the Economic Freedom Fighters (EFF), harnessing the massive discontent among impoverished black South Africans.

In the election of 2014 the EFF captured 6.35 per cent of the vote, becoming the third-largest party in Parliament with a total of twenty-five seats.

Malema, popularly titled Commander-in-Chief of the so-called revolutionary party, stands to attention as he is sworn in as a member of parliament on May 21. He and other EFF MPs, all wearing red miners' overalls, remove their matching hard hats before taking the oath. The female MPs are dressed as cleaning ladies, wearing aprons and headscarves, conveying the clear message that they represent the under-represented: the marginalised and the poor.[2]

The conflict between the EFF and the ANC is ongoing. After his very first speech to Parliament on 18 June 2014, Malema is suspended from the National Assembly after accusing the government of murder in connection with the Marikana Massacre.[3]

In mid-August 2010, forty-four people died at a mine owned by Lonmin in the Marikana area near Rustenburg, among them thirty-four miners shot in a single day by police.[4] The shooting is the worst example of police brutality in South Africa since the end of apartheid and has been compared to the 1960 Sharpeville Massacre, when police killed sixty-nine demonstrators—many of them shot in the back while fleeing. Only this time, both the victims and the perpetrators are black.

14

GOOD FENCES MAKE GOOD NEIGHBOURS

During apartheid the division of South Africans into different racial categories was entrenched through the institution of a series of laws. The Group Areas Act of 1950 established different living spaces for people of different races, and restricted land ownership to your area of residence; each group was to live in its own territory, with its own government. Instituted in the same year, the Immorality Amendment Act prohibited sexual intercourse between white and non-white. Then, in 1953, the Reservation of Separate Amenities Act regulated the segregation of public facilities. Whites and non-whites had to use separate toilets, beaches, parks, buses, cinemas, restaurants, entrances and swimming pools.[1]

'Professional' racial classifiers judged people's appearances and questioned them about their heritage and descent. Social standing and behaviour also played a part, and friends or neighbours could object to an individual's classification, spurring further investigation.

What racial group you ended up in largely shaped the course of your life; not only did it determine where you could live and who you could marry or date, but it determined what schools and universities you could attend, the kind of job for which you qualified, and whether or not you could vote.

By 1956, nearly a hundred thousand 'borderline' cases had been identified, which often resulted in the tragic breaking apart of families. Absurdly enough, your racial classification was not permanent. Every year the government announced how many white people had been reclassified as 'Coloured', how many Coloured people had been reclassified as 'white', and how many Coloured people were now formally regarded as 'African'.[2]

In order to keep the urban black population to a minimum and ensure that cheap labour stayed on the farms, laws were implemented requiring any black person in the city to carry a pass. If they failed to find work that could earn them the right to a pass within seventy-two hours of arriving in the city, they would be forced to leave. Those who did find work were housed in sub-standard hostels, spending most of the year separated from their families. Black farm workers weren't allowed to seek out other work unless a labour bureau in their region confirmed that the labour supply in the district was sufficient. In the cities, 'idle blacks' could be rounded up and forced to work on farms.[3]

Job reservation, or 'civilised labour laws', protected white people from black competition and kept the price of their services artificially high. Pass laws kept black labour costs artificially low, and anti-subversion laws prevented non-whites from forming trade unions. White privilege became the basis on which the National Party could prosper.

While apartheid was an ideology born of the will to survive or, put differently, the fear of extinction, Afrikaner leaders differed on how best to implement it. While some were satisfied with segregationist policies placing them at the top of a social and economic hierarchy, others truly believed in the concept of 'separate but equal'. For the latter, the ideological justification for the classification, segregation, and denial of political rights, was the plan to set aside special land reserves for black South Africans, later called 'bantustans' or 'homelands'. Each ethnic group would have its own state with its own political system and economy, and each would rely on its own labour force. Consequently, South Africa's white population would have to reduce their dependence on black labour and invest in developing the reserves, the apartheid idealists argued. These independent states would then coexist alongside white South Africa in a spirit of friendship and collaboration. In their own areas, black citizens would enjoy full rights.[4]

In 1951, Prime Minister D.F. Malan introduced the Bantu Authorities Act, which saw the setting aside of thirteen per cent of the country's land for the development of 'black homelands'. 'Traditional tribal leaders' were appointed to run the designated homelands, a difficult task considering the widespread poverty, poor soil quality, and lack of infrastructure and services in these areas. In 1950, Professor F.R. Tomlinson, an expert in agricultural economics, had been asked to lead a commission to investigate what it would take to transform the poor and overpopulated reserves into independent and financially viable Bantustans. The Tomlinson Commission delivered its report in 1954 and its findings were a disappointment for the advocates of a so-called ethical apartheid. Immense investments in infrastructure, education, and industry would be needed to make the homelands viable. The cost would be much higher than anticipated, and required significant sacrifices from the white population—which few were willing to make. Thus, the report was conveniently ignored and only a fraction of the needed investments and land set aside.[5] As a result, economic development in the homelands was a disaster. The homelands were not industrialised, nor were jobs created. Black families in larger cities made three to four times as much as families in the homelands. In 1966, the total gross domestic product of all the homelands combined was only 1.9 per cent of South Africa's total GDP. The notion of 'separate but equal' had failed.[6]

16 DECEMBER 1949

THREAT LEVEL: RED

On 16 December 1949, the 40-metre tall, granite Voortrekker Monument opened to the public. The inauguration drew an estimated 250,000 people, the largest crowd the country had ever seen. The design of the building ensures that once a year—at noon on 16 December—the sun hits the opening in the domed ceiling and shines straight down onto a cenotaph, the symbolic resting place of Piet Retief and all the other Voortrekkers who died during the Great Trek. On the grave an inscription reads: *Ons vir jou, Suid-Afrika* (We for thee, South Africa).

It was a great achievement, yet D.F. Malan's speech on the inauguration day was sombre. He warned that the Voortrekker spirit was being undermined by global influences and the communist threat. He urged a return to traditional Voortrekker values.[1]

Surveys from the era show that few white people regarded the rapid population growth among non-whites as a danger to their security and continued dominance. Instead, communism, and African guerrilla movements fighting in its name, were considered the main threats.[2]

'Communism was by far our biggest fear,' says Cecilia Kruger, Chief Professional Officer at the Heritage Foundation in Pretoria. 'We would stash away cans of food. My mom went to weekly preparation meetings to combat the red threat. It was all about the red enemy. We were so preoccupied with this that we forgot about the black enemy. I even had to learn to shoot at fourteen,' she recalls.

In 1950, to combat the so-called *rooi gevaar*, or red menace, Parliament passed the Suppression of Communism Act and banned the Communist Party of South Africa (CPSA). In the 1960s the focus of the communist witch-hunt shifted and became about combating 'the enemy within'—disloyal Afrikaners encouraging active resistance among black citizens.[3]

15

THE REVEREND

Reverend Schalk Albertyn was a 'disloyal' Afrikaner who stood up to the ideology of apartheid in its birthplace—the Dutch Reformed Church. But fighting apartheid was far from the obvious path for him growing up.

'I was brought up in a very conservative house,' he tells me. 'In those days there was only apartheid. At home, in school, everywhere, you were taught that apartheid was right. We all grew up knowing it to be a fact of life that as a white person you are different from a black person because you are civilised, and therefore you shouldn't live among them or even talk to them. The attitude was that they were slaves, although they weren't called that. They were there to take orders. There was no other reality for us.'

It wasn't until university that Albertyn started to question what he had been taught. In the 1970s and 80s there were widespread conflicts between the professors at Stellenbosch who supported apartheid and those who did not. Students like Albertyn got caught in the crossfire and were challenged to question their convictions.

'The anti-apartheid theologians were the most convincing,' he says. 'They advocated a worldview that was not based on separateness and they supplied the theological foundation for that. These professors started bringing people together; they would take the students to Coloured congregations and get people talking to each other.'

After finishing school in his late twenties, Albertyn had to do military service. He enlisted as a preacher in the Air Force. He was sent to the Angolan border where he was responsible for motivating the troops in their fight against the 'enemy': the Angolan government, SWAPO,[1] and their Soviet and Cuban allies.

'Even the preachers who supported apartheid struggled with this because the Bible doesn't call on you to kill others. But it was what was expected of us,' says Albertyn.

So the Reverend tried to be wise and diplomatic in his preaching. He would visit the soldiers in their tents or work areas where they maintained aeroplanes and helicopters.

'I never got into politics. I never tried to convince them of something they didn't want to believe. I just said where I stood and how I believed a Christian should live. Then I left it to them to make up their own minds. Set ideas are hard to change, but if you undermine the theological foundation of the ideology then you can change the mindset without saying anything about the politics.'

'Did it work?' I ask.

'A soldier is a soldier. In the battlefield the training kicks in and you shoot or get shot. Afterwards is when the processing starts. I would like to believe that I made a difference; that I started changing their mindsets. Sometimes wounded SWAPO fighters who were brought in had Bibles in their pockets. This was difficult for the soldiers to understand. Apartheid was a Christian ideology and the soldiers were told they were fighting

anti-Christian communists. Finding well-thumbed Bibles in the
pockets of wounded enemies gave me an opportunity to explain.
It was very confusing for the soldiers to find that the so-called
terrorists were not all anti-Christ and that sometimes the fighting was Christian against Christian.'

In 1981, after completing his military service, Albertyn was
assigned a Christian Indian congregation in Malabar, a suburb of
Port Elizabeth. Back then, it was the job of white ministers like
him to uphold the apartheid structure. The reverend and his
family were sent to live in a whites-only area, and commute the
8 km to Malabar—designated an Indian area—every day. They
did so for the first eight months until Albertyn convinced his
church council to apply for special permission from the minister
of internal affairs for them to live in the strictly Indian area.

The church council worried that their white congregations
would cut off the funding. 'But I promised them that if that
happened I would become a tent-making minister. I would find
another job and finance my own salary,' says Albertyn.

So the council supported his application and he was called in
for a long personal interview where he argued that it was only
proper for a minister to stay with the people to whom he
preaches so that he can be available to them and so that they can
see that he is honest about how he lives. Permission was eventually granted and in 1982 Revd Albertyn claims he became the
first white minister in South Africa to live in a non-white area.

'Everybody came to visit us and bring us presents when we
moved in. They were so happy because to them this was a sign
that we recognised their humanity. They always thought that
white people regarded them as not human enough to live
amongst,' he tells me.

The Indian congregation was too small to support itself, so
the Dutch Reformed Church provided his salary. Soon he was
invited to preach to their other congregations as well, and he

took this opportunity to introduce Indian Christians from his church council to the white congregations.

'This was not always accepted. It was where the conflicts started, but also where the change started,' he says.

Albertyn also invited members from the white congregations to visit the Indian congregation. He gathered ministers from the black and Coloured areas and formed a ministers' fraternity. They'd meet regularly to discuss issues of mutual interest and to preach to each other's congregations. Persuading white congregations to accept a non-white guest preacher was often difficult, but Albertyn slowly made progress. By bringing these people together to talk and share a meal, they eventually learned to accept one another.

'People lived so separately from each other that they didn't know one another. Forcing people together was the only way to break that. Then they would realise, "Oh my word, these people teach their children the same values and think the same way I do; and even if their culture differs from ours, it's not because they are less human,"' he says.

Through the Scripture Union, Albertyn persuaded other white congregation members to become involved. During school holidays mixed-race Bible camps were held, and as more and more people met, perceptions on both sides started to change.

In the 1980s, political violence rose dramatically in South Africa. The ANC launched a campaign to make the townships ungovernable through boycotts and militant action. In response, President P.W. Botha declared a state of emergency in the worst affected parts of the country. By 1986, this state of emergency was extended to include the whole country. The government implemented curfews controlling the movement of people, and it became near impossible for a black person to visit a white area, and vice versa.

Police patrols intensified and community and church leaders were arrested. Albertyn learned that his name was on a list of people the security police planned to arrest. But a prominent security police officer in Port Elizabeth belonged to the same congregation as the reverend's father-in-law, and he convinced the authorities to let him be.

'But my ability to impact change had become limited,' Albertyn remembers.

Life was also becoming increasingly difficult for his wife, Cecilia. She had a job in the city and had to travel through the Coloured areas every day to get to work. Every day, as she entered and then left the secured white area, she was stopped and questioned by the police.

By now there was another white minister in the Indian community: someone whom Albertyn trusted; someone who could take his place. So, when he received a call from a black congregation in Bophuthatswana who needed a minister, Albertyn decided it was time to move on.

Located in the north-western region of South Africa, the Republic of Bophuthatswana was one of ten Bantustans established by the apartheid government. It was granted independence in 1977, one of four states to become nominally independent (a status recognised only by South Africa and other homelands): it was preceded by the Transkei in 1976, and followed shortly by the Ciskei in 1979 and Venda in 1980 (collectively known as the TBVC states). However, independence meant that the people who belonged to these homelands lost their South African citizenship and could be deported. Any funds extended to these newly founded countries were classified as foreign aid by the South African government.[2] On a more positive note, independence from South Africa also meant that people were allowed to live wherever they wanted and associate with whomever they wanted within the confines of their 'homeland'. Revd Albertyn and his family lived in Mafikeng where there was a relatively large white population as the Bophuthatswanan government derived many of its civil servants from South Africa. Bophuthatswana also had a South African embassy.

'Here, white people were more open,' Albertyn recalls. 'These were whites who were already working under black cabinet ministers, for black bosses, or together with blacks in the offices.'

The reverend applied the same strategy as he had in his previous congregation. Here it was much easier to implement, as there were no laws restricting mixed-race interaction.

After two years with the black congregation, Albertyn agreed to transfer to a white congregation. Given the role of the church in shaping the system, he concluded that the dismantling of apartheid should also originate with the church.

'I tried to change people's ideas and show that apartheid goes against the gospel. Not by being an activist in the political sense of the word, but by bringing people together to let them eat and worship together. The apartheid ideology always emphasised the differences, and because of the differences you had to be kept apart. I wanted people to see that we are all just human beings, that there are more points of common ground as Christians than points of difference.'

16 DECEMBER 1961

THE SECOND BATTLE FOR BLOOD RIVER BEGINS

Government buildings blown out; glass, concrete and metal twisted in the streets; mammoth transmission towers brought down like Goliath, now lying helpless on their sides; cables snapped, hanging limply in the air.

On 16 December 1961, the ANC announced the creation of its first armed wing, *Umkhonto we Sizwe*, Spear of the Nation, thereby abandoning their philosophy of non-violence. The leader of *Umkhonto we Sizwe* was none other than Nelson Mandela. The government's massacre of sixty-nine peaceful protestors at Sharpeville and their subsequent banning of the ANC had made it clear that non-violent protest alone would not force the regime to change. In eighteen months the group carried out some 200 acts of sabotage; but the underground organisation was no match for the government regime, which began to employ even harsher methods of repression. Laws were passed to make sabotage punishable by death and to allow police to detain people for ninety days without trial. By 1964 Mandela and other influential ANC leaders had been captured, convicted, and sentenced to life in prison, putting a temporary damper on ANC's armed struggle.

16

TURNING A BLIND EYE

'One issue that deeply worried me in prison was the false image that I unwittingly projected to the outside world; of being regarded as a saint. I never was one, even on the basis of an earthly definition of a saint as a sinner who keeps on trying.'

Nelson Mandela, *Conversations with Myself*

As South Africa's economy modernised, the rate of unemployment among educated black citizens soared from 3 per cent in 1960 to 93 per cent in 1990. With rising unemployment came rising desperation and the escalation of violence. In the Soweto uprising of 1976 many protestors were either students or unemployed.[1]

During this period, the ANC scored some major diplomatic victories, garnering significant international support as they successfully lobbied for economic sanctions. They also intensified their armed struggle. Between 1976 and 1983 the ANC carried out 362 acts of violence. ANC guerrillas struck at some high-profile targets, including a military base in Pretoria, a nuclear reactor near Cape Town, and the Air Force headquarters in Pretoria where a car bomb killed nineteen people.[2] These armed attacks were combined with mass campaigns of civil disobedience aimed at making the townships ungovernable.

But not all freedom fighters agreed with the chosen tactics or supported the level of violence. The Inkatha Freedom Party (IFP) and its leader Mangosuthu Buthelezi, Chief Minister of the KwaZulu homeland in Natal, thought that the armed struggle and sanctions were destroying the chance for peaceful change. He was quickly branded a counter-revolutionary and the relationship between the IFP and the ANC deteriorated.[3]

In 1984 the ANC organised a mass uprising against apartheid. It lasted until the middle of 1986 and by the end the organisation had succeeded in establishing itself as the dominant opposition force,[4] having engaged in bloody feuds with other black liberation movements such as the IFP and the Azanian People's Organisation (AZAPO). Ultimately, the 'black-on-black' struggle claimed thousands of lives, almost three times as many as those taken by the security forces.[5]

However, international media downplayed, or even ignored, this side of the ANC. It appeared inconceivable to most Western media that an organisation like the ANC, a beacon of hope and righteousness, should be implicated in the use of morally questionable tactics.

One example is in the profiling of Winnie Mandela who was internationally hailed as a heroine. In the eyes of the West she was deemed the selfless mother of a nation—a woman who commanded enormous respect and admiration. Meanwhile, back in South Africa, she was implicated in all sorts of trouble.

In 1986, Winnie returned from the Free State to Soweto, defying her banishment by the South African government. There she provided assistance to struggling youth, offering them shelter at her home in return for protection. These youth came to be known as the Mandela United Football Club and started what residents describe as a 'reign of terror' in Soweto. In the late

1980s Winnie Mandela and her 'bodyguards' were implicated directly and indirectly in a wide range of assaults, abductions, murders and attempted murders of people they thought to be traitors of the revolution. In one case, two of these guards used a knife and sulphuric acid from a car battery to carve M for Mandela and VIVA ANC into the flesh of two young suspected informers.[6] Winnie Mandela's guards also stood trial on accusations ranging from rape to murder. Yet it took years for international media to begin reporting accurately on these events. When the family of a teenage girl who had been raped by Mandela's bodyguards burnt down her house in retaliation, most media neglected to report on the reasons. Some media outlets, like the American broadcasting company NBC, even chose to blame the assault on the apartheid regime.[7]

In 1991, Winnie Mandela was found guilty of having been complicit in the kidnapping and beating of four youths who had fallen out with the ANC. One of these youths, fourteen-year-old Stompie Seipei, died from his injuries. The court sentenced Winnie Mandela to six years in prison. Her conviction on charges of accessory to assault was overturned on appeal, but the conviction for kidnapping remained. Still riding on the release of her husband from jail, Winnie managed to fight her way back to political prominence, though her reputation would never be the same.

In 1997, the Truth and Reconciliation Commission (TRC) found Winnie Mandela guilty of playing a part in the murder of Seipei. The TRC was a court-like restorative justice body established in 1996, where victims of human rights violations during apartheid could share their experiences and perpetrators of violence could give testimony and request amnesty from prosecution.

Few media outlets have enough time or resources to provide context to remote conflicts. Oversimplified, they are often assigned a 'good side' and a 'bad side', a villain and a hero. Anything that doesn't fit that narrative is omitted. As a consequence, black-on-black violence during the freedom struggle was almost completely ignored by international media outlets.

Despite their efforts, the apartheid regime failed miserably in their international propaganda efforts. Rian Malan argues that the South African government did such a poor job in this regard that it was equated with Nazi Germany. Few of its redeeming actions ever reached the rest of the world and nothing it said was ever believed. Under the lead of Colonel Vic McPherson, a supposed propaganda 'mastermind', the apartheid government lost complete credibility. The strategic communication efforts of the ANC, on the other hand, were hugely successful. The written word was an important weapon in the struggle against apartheid and many journalists who sympathised with the movement used their positions to further the ANC's propaganda objectives.[8]

I ask Tim du Plessis, who worked as a journalist during apartheid and who, at the time of writing, heads up the Afrikaans newspaper division at Media24,[9] if he thinks the ANC got off too lightly.

'International media cut them a lot of slack,' he tells me. 'The ANC were such good communicators: in exile; in London; in the Scandinavian countries. Mbeki was at the forefront of this. They cultivated an image of themselves that took root, especially in England. Newspapers like *The Guardian* were outright supporters of them, as were the Scandinavian countries and the US. Even now, Western media could be far more critical.'

Rian Malan has studied the Western media's coverage of South Africa both during and after apartheid. In *My Traitor's Heart*, first published in 1990, he uses a poignant example taken from *The New York Times*, 15 April 1986. The top of the page is devoted to a fourteen-inch story about Desmond Tutu's election as Archbishop of Cape Town:

Beneath the Tutu story is a minute headline reading, 'Eleven Die in Night of Violence,' and a squib of copy summarising the government's overnight 'unrest report.' The police shot and killed five black people, and six anonymous burned bodies were found. And *beneath* that, unheralded by any headline, are two cryptic little sentences about the discovery, in a place called Sekhukuniland, of something horrible beyond comprehension: the remains of thirty-two African women, hurled alive into pits of flame. This was the worst mass murder in South African history, and it took place in a context that the *Times* clearly could not bring itself to explain. The seventy-six black youths arrested in connection with the massacre were all members or supporters of the UDF— the supposedly nonviolent liberation movement led by the Nobel Peace Laureate at the head of the page. The thirty-two victims were suspected of using sorcery to retard the freedom struggle, and were incinerated in the name of fundamental change.[10]

17

DINA AT THE MONUMENT

During the second half of the 1980s, an increasing number of South African newspapers began to criticise apartheid. Many were censored or shut down, but in the end it was a pornographic magazine that took on the government censorship board and brought down the last pillar of the regime.

In the early 1990s, music producer Joe Theron decided to enter the sex entertainment industry. He wanted to start publishing *Hustler* in South Africa, so he flew to Los Angeles in an effort to obtain the rights. After trying unsuccessfully for three weeks to get an audience with American porn king Larry Flynt he decided to get more creative. He went to the offices of *Hustler* and rode the elevator up and down until Flynt finally entered the elevator in his wheelchair. After delivering what was quite literally an elevator pitch, Flynt invited Theron into his office. At the end of the meeting, Flynt called his driver and asked him to take Theron back to his hotel to pick up his things, and then drive him to the Flynt mansion. He spent a week there, at the end of which Flynt gave him the rights to publish *Hustler* in South Africa, as well as in all other English-speaking countries outside the US.

In 1993, Theron launched *Hustler* in South Africa. It quickly grew to have the second-largest circulation in the country, although it was four times the price of any other magazine. With sales averaging 200,000 copies a month, Theron became a rich man.

But it wasn't all smooth sailing. Pornography was banned during the apartheid era under the same strict censorship laws that targeted communist and anti-apartheid writings. After the fall of apartheid, the standards were applied less restrictively, but *Hustler* was still repeatedly banned.

'The old censorship laws of South Africa were very old fashioned,' says Theron. 'When we launched *Hustler* in South Africa, we immediately started getting lawsuits against us. The main concern of the judges was the impact on children. We told them that we don't make the magazine for kids; it's for adults.'

Although most bans were lifted on appeal, the constant court hearings were time consuming and frustrating.

'If you came to South Africa from overseas with a *Hustler* magazine in your bag you could go to jail. Yet, I had travelled all over the West and seen porn available in First World countries everywhere.'

After having been dragged to court ten times, and having won all ten times, Theron decided it was time to take on the censorship board. He was eventually granted a session with the head of the board, Braam Coetzee, who would in turn decide whether or not Theron should have the opportunity to appear in front of the entire board.

Theron arrived early for his meeting with Coetzee. He wandered the 22-storey building and learned that there were 186 people working for the censorship board. When he walked into the meeting, he had only two questions:

'Why don't you want grown-ups to read these magazines?'

Coetzee: 'Because it makes them depraved and corrupt.'

'Then aren't you scared to come to work every morning?'

Coetzee: 'Why should I be?'

'Well, you sit here on the twenty-second floor of a building that is filled with 186 people who spend their days reading this stuff.'

Theron was eventually granted his meeting with the censorship board and its nine judges. He turned to one of the judges, an old lady, and asked what training she had received to avoid becoming depraved and corrupt through the material she spent her days reading.

'Well, I'm an old retired school teacher,' she replied.

He went on to pose this question to the other judges and, as expected, none of them had received any special training. They were just ordinary South Africans, and it soon became hard for them to argue that they would be less susceptible to depravity and corruption than any of their fellow countrymen.

A couple of months later Theron received a phone call from Coetzee thanking him for granting him early retirement.

'We closed down the censorship board,' says Theron. 'We changed the whole law here. We set precedent with regard to the sex industry. Censorship was the last pillar of apartheid.'

Theron then helped craft the new censorship laws for South Africa. By then he was publishing *Hustler* in England, Australia and New Zealand. His lawyers submitted proposals for new censorship laws modelled after the English and Australian versions that were by and large accepted.

But laws and value systems are two very different things. While the law henceforth allowed for previously prohibited material, such as pornography, the Afrikaner culture remained unconvinced.

In 1995, Joe launched an Afrikaans version of *Hustler* called *Loslyf*, slang for a promiscuous woman. It was the first ever Afrikaans-language pornographic publication. The first issue featured Dina at the Monument: a topless Afrikaans woman posing in front of the Voortrekker Monument. The issue caused an outcry among the Afrikaner community—and sold an astounding 80,000 copies.

Some seventeen years later, when I enter the *Loslyf* office in downtown Johannesburg, business is significantly slower. As is the case for many printed publications these days, *Loslyf* is finding it hard to compete against web-based alternatives.

Like a wall of fame, old covers from the magazine's heyday adorn the long hallway leading to the office of *Loslyf* editor Donovan van Wyngaard. The covers boast poor quality photographs of women wearing the high-cut underwear typical of the 1990s. They would not be considered especially attractive by today's standards.

Although pornography still manages to outrage the conservative Afrikaner community, the novelty of Afrikaner porn has subsided. Van Wyngaard is also convinced that the Afrikaner aversion for pornography is completely feigned.

'The Afrikaner community loves me behind closed doors but hates me in public. They'll hide their *Loslyf* inside their Bible,' he says.

Despite this, Van Wyngaard believes the Afrikaner man has become more sophisticated: 'He is no longer a khaki-clad man in short pants with a firearm by his side. I want the magazine to reflect that change. I want to communicate that I know you're not as idiotic as we thought before,' he says.

In practice that means buying higher-end photographs from America and presenting them as local talent. In reality, only about thirty per cent of the women who appear in the magazine are Afrikaans-speaking.

Van Wyngaard used to work in television but lost his job due to cutbacks. Now, both he and his wife work at *Loslyf.* Although Van Wyngaard is less than six months on the job, he tells me that he has already received death threats.

'My family has completely disowned me and my brother won't speak to me. We didn't end up in this industry by choice, but because of financial strain,' he says.

But somehow I'm finding it hard to believe that it was Joe Theron who corrupted Van Wyngaard and his wife. They are by no means new to the business. In 2009 they produced and marketed the very first pornographic movie in Afrikaans, *Kwaai Naai* or 'The Incredible Screw', which Van Wyngaard claims sold extremely well, somewhere between 10,000 and 15,000 copies. Then came the sequel, *'n Pomp in Elke Dorp*, 'A Shag in Each Town', where a lookalike of a well-known Afrikaans singer and womaniser, Steve Hofmeyr, plays the lead. This was followed by *Amor—'n Bok vir Sports*, a story about a rugby player who cheats on his wife and gets caught on tape. More recently the Van Wyngaards have embarked on a daring, mixed-race production called *Forbidden Times*, supposedly South Africa's first mixed-race porn movie. But the success of the first film has been hard to replicate, he confesses; it is difficult to produce quality on a limited budget.

As I'm preparing to leave, Van Wyngaard pulls me aside. 'Here, take this,' he says as he hands me a copy of *The Girls of the Loslyf Mansion*.

I look at him a little bewildered, and he quickly adds: 'It also contains an interview sequence with Joe discussing censorship in South Africa.'

Joe Theron, founder of *Loslyf* and champion of South African pornography, walks into the room. When he notices the movie in my hand he frowns, visibly displeased.

'I thought it might interest her to see your interview,' Van Wyngaard comments.

But Theron ignores him and turns to me with stern instructions: 'Make sure you put it away so that people don't see it and get the wrong idea.'

'And that's coming from the owner?' I retort.

He pretends he hasn't heard me, but his tone of voice softens a little.

'Here, let me tell you what you must do.' He takes the DVD, strips its cover and puts it back with the reverse, blank side, facing out. 'There you go. You wouldn't want people to get the wrong idea,' he says.

18

THE BEGINNING OF THE END

By 1978, the National Party and the Broederbond were divided between the so-called *verligtes* and *verkramptes*, the enlightened and closed-minded members. In 1982, Andries Treurnicht, chairman of the Broederbond between 1972 and 1974, broke away to form the Conservative Party (CP). He and most other conservative leaders left the Broederbond. The deep split in the Bond and the loss of many prominent members meant that the influence of the organisation started to wane. However, the loss of its more right-wing members also meant that those remaining were free to start the transition away from old-style apartheid towards preparing the Afrikaner *volk* for inevitable change.

The Broederbond suggested that the National Party would be wise to abolish some key apartheid laws. By late 1984, the widespread civil disobedience and escalating violence still showed no signs of abating. So, in 1985, the National Party government lifted the ban on mixed marriages and sex across the colour bar. A year later, influx control was scrapped. However, nothing was done to accommodate black political aspirations. The country's reputation was shattered, and the rest of the world had little faith in

P.W. Botha's ability to bring about change. Financial sanctions and international isolation soon caused the rand to collapse.

In 1986, the Broederbond drafted a document called *Basiese staatkundige voorwaardes vir die voortbestaan van die Afrikaner* ('Basic Constitutional Conditions for the Survival of the Afrikaner'). It stated that the situation had become unsustainable and that all South Africans had to have equal human and civil rights. But the motivation for this had little to do with morality. The only way to survive, the document stated, was to share power with black South Africans instead of excluding them. Power-sharing should be done in such a way so that no one group could dominate another. A negotiated settlement focusing on minority rights was deemed to be the way forward.

Gaining acceptance for the document required much legwork. Members of the Broederbond toured the country to convince community leaders that a negotiated solution was the way to proceed. The selected community leaders were then asked to spread the word within their spheres of influence.

In an interview with South African journalist Max du Preez, Pieter de Lange, then chairman of the Afrikaner Broederbond spoke of his involvement in these negotiations:

> The National Party had nothing to do with this. It was a secret internal AB project with only a few people at a time being addressed. [...]
>
> So we got through to the more conscious Afrikaners and planted the idea of a negotiated settlement. Sensible people knew that it was a choice between a bloodbath or the end of apartheid and a negotiated, peaceful transition. [...]
>
> I organised two workshops (*dinkskrums*) with the military and some of the top minds during that time. The conclusion was that we could have maintained the status quo with our military for a long time, even after bankruptcy. But by the end of the 1990s everything would have collapsed. We would have started killing each other in the streets. Now, if the best brains in the country tell you this and you still want to continue, then you must be very stupid.[1]

16 DECEMBER 1988

TAINTED STORY, FADING GLORY

On the 150th anniversary of the Battle of Blood River, another big reenactment was planned. However, this time attendance was meagre: apartheid was ending and nationalism considered unfashionable.

'By the end of the 1980s the National Party was rudderless, leaderless and bereft of ideas, much like the ANC today. Academia, churches and newspapers became critical, partly because they realised the game was up and partly because they realised it was inherently wrong,' says Tim du Plessis.

By now the media had evolved into a moral compass for Afrikaners, communicating the unpleasant, and initially unpopular, message that the system was wrong and in need of change.

'We played a part in the transformation, but it cannot take away from the fact that we supported apartheid for decades; that we helped keep the system in place,' says Du Plessis.

In the 1960s, *Die Burger* voiced its first dissenting opinion when it questioned the government's decision to strip Coloured people in the Western Cape of the right to vote.[1]

'It took us fifteen years to question the fundamentals. It took the black journalists less than three years before they started to criticise the ANC. I admire that. Many of them grew up in ANC homes, just like we grew up in National Party homes. Still, they broke ranks and started criticising,' says Du Plessis.

A journalist since 1976, Du Plessis has worked almost exclusively in the Afrikaans press.

'Working as a reporter during apartheid was complicated and simple at the same time. We worked fairly freely as journalists and were able to write whatever we wanted, but we knew that we worked for a newspaper that during elections would endorse the party,' he tells me.

Although not directly funded by the party, the Afrikaans newspapers largely supported apartheid policy and the National Party, acting as part of the system designed to keep the electorate convinced.

The South African Broadcasting Corporation (SABC) had a monopoly on all radio and television broadcasts until the late 1980s. It was entirely controlled by the Broederbond who used it to promote the organisation's interests, and its board and management were made up mainly of its members. Afrikaans channels were used to advance the aims of the National Party and Afrikaner nationalism, while the so-called Bantu Services were supposed to boost the benefits of the Bantustans.

The Broederbond's secret document, *Masterplan for a White Country: the Strategy*, outlined the importance of using media to achieve political objectives and more specifically to 'compel' the black population to live and work in their own homelands as soon as possible.[2]

'We even had cultural commissars in our society—kind of like cultural guardians—who would go around and say what a good

Afrikaner should be like and what he should think,' says Du Plessis.

He's amused when I tell him that these days it is difficult to find Afrikaners willing to acknowledge that they supported apartheid.

'Rubbish!' he says. 'They all supported it. We all grew up in Afrikaner homes; we all came from Afrikaans schools; we accepted the system.'

Du Plessis entered university with little more than a vague feeling of unease about the political status quo. He didn't start questioning it until he started working as a journalist at *Beeld* in 1976.

'That's when I first heard Soweto leaders like Tutu and Buthelezi speak, and became exposed to the realities. It was the year of the Soweto riots. The paper was mildly critical of the government's handling of the rebellion, but only mildly,' he reveals.

By the mid-1980s, Du Plessis was reporting critically minded articles himself.

'I was critical, but within confinements. I never questioned the last "whites only" election in 1989, but by then everybody could see the game was over.'

From 1984 onwards, Du Plessis was in regular contact with ANC leaders. Willem Wepener, then editor of *Beeld*, would send him to places such as Zambia to meet with banned leaders in exile, like Thabo Mbeki. Their quotes would then be attributed to non-banned—and, as Du Plessis puts it, 'less clever'—ANC members in South Africa. It was also Wepener who popped the big question a few years later when, in a famous 1988 editorial, he questioned whether the time hadn't yet come to release Nelson Mandela from prison.

Although the elite had started to realise that change was inevitable, the average Afrikaner was far from ready to hand over power.

Many feared recrimination, discrimination and retaliation, and support for right-wing parties began to rise again. According to a poll conducted in 1988, only 1 per cent of Afrikaners and 3 per cent of English-speakers wanted to see Nelson Mandela in power. A mere 3 per cent of Afrikaners said they found majority control acceptable. Even the younger generation was largely negative. In 1989 nearly half of Afrikaner students said that they would physically resist an ANC-controlled government. Another third stated that they would simply emigrate.[3]

The majority of Afrikaners consistently rejected giving up more 'white' land for the development of the reserves, beyond the 13 per cent already set aside. Life was good and few were inclined to make sacrifices in order to attempt to provide an ethical foundation for their political ideology. Few people realised how fast and how drastically the demographics were shifting. The black population was growing at a rate that no one had anticipated.[4] The increasing demand among black South Africans for political and economic power, together with their strong international support, could no longer be ignored. Soon, white people would be faced with two options: to mobilise for a full-scale war or to seek a compromise through negotiation.[5]

* * *

In December 1989, shortly after he was made president, F.W. de Klerk began a process of major transformation. Under his lead, the ANC and other liberation movements were unbanned and many of apartheid's laws were abolished. All-party negotiations for a new constitution were initiated and in 1990 Nelson Mandela was finally released from prison.

In March 1992, a referendum on reform was held among the white electorate, with the aim of negotiating a new constitution. A surprising 69 per cent of the electorate voted Yes despite the fact that only 15 per cent of the white population believed that they would be better off in a so-called new South Africa. Although most white people realised that their days of privilege were over, and supported surrendering before they could be defeated, few expected the handover of power to be quite so unconditional. Fear was widespread and weapon ownership was at an all-time high, averaging one firearm per white adult.[6]

On 27 April 1994, South Africa held its first racially-inclusive democratic election. The ANC won sixty-two per cent of the votes. And on 10 May 1994, Nelson Mandela was inaugurated as South Africa's first black president, with De Klerk serving alongside Thabo Mbeki as a deputy in the new Government of National Unity. The world cheered and hailed as a miracle what was proudly known as the Rainbow Nation.

This unity, however, was short-lived. During the pre-1994 negotiations, representatives of the National Party and the ANC had agreed upon the framework for a new constitution. But in 1996, when the new constitution was actually drafted, the ANC refused to accept a power-sharing cabinet. Feeling betrayed, De Klerk pulled the National Party out of government and, as a result, the first Government of National Unity collapsed, leaving the white community without any formal political power.[7] This had an immense impact on the attitudes of white South Africans. While in 1992 only four per cent of Afrikaners regarded South Africa as a country that was, first and foremost, for black people, and one where they would have to accept second place, in 1998 that number had grown to forty-three per cent.[8]

19

THE REVEREND LOSES HIS FLOCK

As apartheid was coming to an end, war broke out in the homeland of Bophuthatswana. President Lucas Mangope was not interested in joining an integrated South Africa; and, in March 1994, conflict erupted between those who were loyal to Mangope and those who wished to be part of the new South Africa. Reintegrationists called for Bophuthatswana to be annexed against their president's wishes. Rumours spread that ANC supporters were getting ready to move in. Riots broke out, spiralled out of control, and the president fled the country.

In a last desperate attempt to remain independent, Mangope turned to General Constand Viljoen, former head of the South African Army and leader of the all-white Afrikaner Volksfront. Mangope asked the general for military assistance to keep the ANC from reintegrating the homeland by force. Viljoen and his organisation responded to the call. However, members of Volksfront's ally, the ultra-right-wing Afrikaner Weerstands-beweging (AWB) also arrived. As a well-known extremist group, they were not welcome.

'The AWB thought that they had to save Bophuthatswana and came in to make war. There was a whole revolution. Bophuthatswana's defence force and police force tried to drive out the AWB. They shot each other in the streets. Then the South African Defence Force moved in,' Revd Schalk Albertyn remembers.

The rest is television history, as news cameras caught the light-blue Mercedes of three AWB members being riddled with bullets. The car came to a halt, but only once the driver had been fatally wounded. The injured passengers crawled out. Wounded and bleeding, they threw themselves on the ground, arms in the air, and pleaded for mercy. Then a Bophuthatswana police constable stepped up and executed them, in front of the rolling cameras. The incident was widely broadcast. The apartheid diehards had been defeated; and their bloody, khaki-clad bodies, lying limp on a dusty street in Bophuthatswana, became a symbol of the death of apartheid.

Then, after the election of 1994, Bophuthatswana suddenly ceased to exist, its territory divided up between the provinces of the Northern Cape and the Northwest. The new South African government withdrew all its civil servants from Bophuthatswana with immediate effect.

'The civil servants made up most of my congregation,' says Albertyn. 'We went from over a thousand members to around five hundred members in a day or two. There wasn't much of a future.'

Although Mangope is sometimes described as an unpopular autocrat, Bophuthatswana was one of few viable homelands and the Revd has only positive things to say about his years there.

'The place was thriving,' he tells me. 'Over 50 per cent of the budget was spent on education and health. Not all the homelands worked properly, but Bophuthatswana definitely did. People wanted to remain separate and so they supported apartheid as a structure. It didn't fit well with the ANC's ideas of coming to save them. They didn't want to be saved.'

At this point the church had two ministers, but after the sudden loss of so many members, Revd Albertyn knew the congregation wouldn't be able to afford them both. Being the more senior of the two, Albertyn suspected he would be asked to stay. The other minister had just married and had a newborn baby. If he lost his job it would be difficult for him to support his family, so Albertyn decided to resign before the church asked one of them to leave.

Since he left in the midst of all the upheaval caused by the dismantling of apartheid, Albertyn knew that receiving a new posting might take a while, but he wasn't prepared for just how long. There was an oversupply of ministers and fewer postings to go around because of the change in government. While he remained a church council member, still preaching occasionally, he had no way of making a living. He tried farming; he opened a diving business; but in the end, unable to make ends meet, he started working at the grocery stores Spar and Pick n Pay.

While Albertyn didn't ever stop applying for church positions, after eight years without success, he couldn't help but feel disappointed in the church for having abandoned him.

'At some point I began to feel bitterness towards the church. I felt that I still had something to give and that they didn't want me,' he says.

16 DECEMBER 1998

MUSEUM-JACKING

'History constitutes a discussion without end. Past reality is not possible but only a reconstructed, socially created knowledge. [...] many "truths" are possible in the production of history and none deserves to be silenced.'

From *Ncome/Blood River: Another Point of View*

On 16 December 1998, ANC leaders, including Thabo Mbeki, then deputy president, held an earth-turning ceremony to celebrate the construction of a new heritage site directly across the river from the Afrikaner museum at Blood River.

The original idea was to build a memorial and a cultural centre that would provide a more neutral representation of the battle; it would focus on honouring the dead. But by the time the museum was completed in 1999, a shift in politics had caused a change in focus. The planned wall of remembrance was scrapped and the emphasis went from honouring the dead to reinterpreting history—highlighting the warrior heritage of the Zulu people. The outcome was a museum modelled after the Zulu war formation, 'the horns of the bull', with interconnected buildings laid out to form a head, chest and two horns. The museum exterior was decorated with designs from Zulu warrior shields.[1]

The exhibits themselves focus on Zulu culture and warrior practices, emphasising the legacy of King Dingaan and his lineage of Zulu kings. Here, 16 December is described as the day on which 'the Zulu nation displayed great bravery in defending their homeland'.[2] The portrayal of the battle itself is radically different from the version depicted across the river. At the Ncome museum, the Voortrekkers are portrayed as the initial aggressors, and the Zulu attack is thereby justified as a form of self-defence. The curators question the historical accuracy of nearly every aspect of the Afrikaner legend. While the Afrikaner museum suggests that when Piet Retief and his men went to see Dingaan, the king had already agreed to give the trekkers land, the Ncome museum suggests that this could not have been the case: according to Zulu traditions, land was indivisible and new people who wanted to reside on it were required to ask permission from the local *induna* who would then consult the king. The trekkers ignored this procedure and, as a result, were seen by the Zulu people as invaders.[3]

The exhibit at the Ncome museum suggests that the document supposedly retrieved from the body of Piet Retief could in fact have been a fraud. The body had been exposed to the elements for some time before the trekkers found it. Wouldn't any document have disintegrated? they ask. And if there was a treaty, did Dingaan actually sign it? Was he even literate; would he have been able to understand the contents of a treaty? And on it goes. Everything down to the weather conditions on the day of the battle is debated. Even the fundamental spiritual foundation of Blood River is challenged, suggesting that the Vow to God was not made until after the battle had taken place.

A sign on a wall of the Ncome museum proclaims:

> The Zulu people are a proud nation who know how to reconcile with each other or with an enemy after a confrontation. [...] The descendants of the original protagonists at the battle of Ncome/Blood River, namely the Zulus and Afrikaners of today, are no longer enemies, but jointly participating in preserving the monuments of the sites, promoting a spirit of reconciliation and building a united South Africa.

20

THE BROTHERS OF SUNSHINE CORNER

At the end of a long dirt road, just far enough from Pretoria to be ignored by the city's Department of Public Works, sits the township of Sunshine Corner. The familiar signs of semi-rural African poverty punctuate the scene: tyres, chickens and old broken furniture litter the dirt pathways between the buildings. The shacks are patchworks of wood, sheet metal and cardboard. Tarpaulins, held in place by stones, provide meagre shelter from rain.

As I walk the streets, a door suddenly swings open on broken hinges. In the opening of a ramshackle dwelling, no bigger than a garden shed, I'm greeted by a short young man, with bright, friendly eyes. His name is Kobus Gouws, he is twenty-nine years old and lives here with his twenty-six-year-old stepbrother, Casper Muller. Sunshine Corner is a white township.

Inside their house, the temperature is quickly approaching unbearable as the sun reaches for its high-noon mark. Three cots with broken frames and collapsed springs take up most of the floor space in the one-room shack. Sunlight seeps through the cracks between the wooden slats that make up the walls, pouring in through those places where the slats have broken. Two of the beds belong to the brothers and the third to a friend of theirs who is rarely around. A sheet hangs across the shack in an attempt to create some privacy for the friend. Together, they share the place with three cats: Fluffy and her 2-month-old kittens, Patches and Blackie. The place reeks of cat urine.

The brothers are visibly dirty. Kobus apologises for their appearance, brushing off his comic book T-shirt and tucking it into his baggy blue shorts. There is a communal shower but he says that they don't have money for soap or toiletries. The room itself is worse: crayon scribbles cover the walls; cat hair and dirt line most of the surfaces. Yet, in spite of this, everything is carefully organised. The cots are neatly made, old woolen blankets pulled tightly across them. Buckets, glasses and sticks, and the rest of their few possessions, are all stacked away in corners or under beds. Like children cleaning a treehouse, the big things are all attended to, while the odours go unnoticed.

Unlike his slight, older stepbrother, Casper is tall, strong and broad shouldered. But between the faraway look in his eyes and his flaccid cheeks, you quickly get the sense that he is not nearly as intellectually developed as he is physically. Kobus explains that Casper had a stroke when he was sixteen, leaving him with the mental capacity of a seven-year-old.

'This is my bed,' says Casper proudly, pointing to the middle cot where a small white teddy bear with a pink bow rests against the pillow. Over the old, white, metal headboard hangs a picture of Miley Cyrus, the actress of Hannah Montana fame and a childhood idol of young girls around the world.

'She's pretty,' says Casper, smiling shyly.

We sit down—Casper on his bed, Kobus on the only chair and I on the friend's bed. I notice a set of names tattooed roughly in large black letters on Kobus's arms and legs: LOUISE, RICARDO, ELOZINE.

'Ricardo is my son. He's 16. Elozine, she's 13. And Louise is their mom. She lives in Plettenberg,' Kobus explains.

Kobus himself looks barely 16, but at just 29 years old, I conclude that he must have fathered Ricardo at the age of 12 or 13.

'So you have two kids?' I ask.

'No, three. The youngest is Tandi. She is seven. But they all live with their mom.'

'Doesn't Tandi get a tattoo?' I ask.

'Yeah, I suppose it's her turn next.'

'Are you saving up?'

'No, I do them myself. With melted rubber,' Kobus explains.

I notice the tops of letters sticking out just above Casper's shirt.

'Do you have a tattoo too?' I ask Casper.

He hesitates, then nods and pulls down his T-shirt to show me. There, tattooed across the top of his chest, in clear but childishly uneven script is THE DEVIL.

I don't know what to say; I turn to Kobus for an explanation. Who would do this to Casper? Why? To humiliate him? To mark him as an outcast? I know that in some African cultures people with mental disabilities are thought to be possessed. But Kobus's face remains unaltered, offering no clue.

I turn back to face Casper.

'When they hit me. At school. I didn't want them to hit me more,' he tells me in slow, broken speech. 'Then I got this tattoo. Everybody knows the Devil. Everybody is scared of him.'

I glance back at Kobus, who nods.

'They hit Kobus too,' Casper adds. He leans forward, half-whispering, 'So he called himself Satan.'

Kobus seems a little embarrassed by the story, but he reaches out lovingly and pats his brother on the arm.

'But we're okay now, aren't we,' he says.

* * *

Kobus has been trying for years to secure a disability pension for Casper, but without any success. Casper's mental disability should be immediately apparent to anyone who meets him, but the brothers have no medical record of the stroke, so he simply does not qualify for assistance.

'We have lots of cases like that,' says Mariana Kriel, regional manager at Helping Hand, a charity organisation helping destitute Afrikaners. 'The government won't recognise disability in whites. It's definitely a race issue.'

Kriel explains that only medical assessments conducted by government doctors are recognised. However, securing an appointment with an approved doctor is difficult, especially if you're white, she claims.

There are about four hundred white squatter camps in South Africa, Kriel informs me. 'And that's just the ones we at Helping Hand know about. We are not represented everywhere, so there are likely more.'

According to Christine Breet, Deputy Executive Director of Development at Helping Hand, approximately 600,000 of South Africa's 3 million Afrikaners live below the poverty line. In 2008 that figure was 420,000.

'Affirmative action has had a very negative impact on the white community, but white poverty is very un-PC. It is not the politically correct thing to talk about,' says Breet.

Helping Hand defines poverty as any household with a joint income of less than 3,000 rand a month. However, it is important to emphasise that this is Helping Hand's own metric for poverty. Other South African organisations put the poverty line at 500 rand a month—a line that includes millions of black families, but comparatively few white ones. Obviously, where the limit is set significantly influences the political impact of the statistics.

The existence of white poverty in South Africa is a highly contested issue. While the fact remains that, overall, white South Africans are less affected by poverty and unemployment than their black counterparts, there is a prevailing conviction among the majority that all white people are wealthy—a misconception largely shared by the ANC leadership. Confronted with a statement that there had been a 30 per cent increase in white people being counted as among the poorest of the poor, former president Mbeki replied that he found it 'very encouraging' that income disparity between white and black was now levelling out.[1]

In 2008, the *Mail & Guardian* ran a story on President Zuma's surprise when Helping Hand escorted him out to visit some of the country's white squatter camps. 'I did not know there were poor whites,' he allegedly exclaimed.

Hans Duvenhage owns the little patch of land and accompanying shacks that comprise Sunshine Corner. He has been living here for twenty-five years, renting out shacks since 1997.

'In the first month I had 180 people show up,' he tells me.

Over time the number of tenants stabilised around a hundred. The rent is 400 rand per shack per month, which includes breakfast and supper. But according to Duvenhage, only seven of the current 110 residents actually pay this fee, so the community relies on food donations to survive. Pick n Pay Centurion donates sugar, bread, vegetables and washing powder to the community.

Some of the residents work as gardeners, car guards or parking lot attendants to earn a living. About twenty per cent of the population has some sort of job in Centurion, the nearest city to Sunshine Corner. Many of the rest are pensioners. As there is no municipal public transit outside urban areas, the community is very isolated. The cost of the series of minibus taxis needed to get all the way to Centurion is too expensive for most residents to afford.

At the time of writing, there are thirty-three children living in Sunshine Corner, but because of the transportation issues, few of the children of Sunshine Corner make it past primary school. The nearest high school is in Pretoria North—about fifteen kilometres away.

'Can't the kids walk or bike?' I ask Mariana Kriel of Helping Hand.

'Try to bike and you don't know if you are coming back. The area is very unsafe,' she replies.

Residents say that even the relatively short walk to the nearest grocery store, which takes you along an unlit gravel road, is unsafe. Kriel says there have been many incidents of assault and rape as residents of Sunshine Corner make their way to and from the little store, especially on pension day—the 15th of every month—when the township's elderly men and women receive their monthly 1,200 rand check.

To my surprise, there are two black families living in the township. They are not around during my visit, and I'm told that they 'keep to themselves'. I can't help but think that the architects of apartheid would be pleased to know that South Africa's white poor, considered the most prone to racial mixing, remain largely segregated, their beds well made.

Most of the squatter camps are situated on private property and consist of a gathering of Wendy houses and tents. Even where electricity is available, it is far from reliable and few can afford it. Instead, most people use coal and gas to cook.

Finding enough work to survive is hard, says Kobus. He tells me that he goes to Centurion to wash cars. Yesterday he made 50 rand: enough to cover the bus ride to the city and back, a meal and a cool drink. While that day he ate, in the evening he was back at the camp with nothing to show for his efforts.

21

AFFIRMATIVE ACTION

In 2005 police captain Renate Barnard applied for a job as a superintendent. She was tested, interviewed and recommended for the position. The selection committee found that the difference between Barnard's scores and that of the only black candidate to make the shortlist was so great that service delivery would be compromised if he was appointed to the post. However, the divisional commissioner was unwilling to appoint a white candidate, and so decided that the post should be left vacant.[1]

A year later, the post was advertised again, and again Barnard applied. A selection panel once again identified her as the only suitable candidate. This time even the divisional commissioner recommended that she should get the job. But Jackie Selebi, then Chief of Police, rejected her appointment on the basis that it would not promote affirmative action. The post was advertised for the third time, but when Barnard applied once more, it was withdrawn.[2/3]

Barnard responded by taking her employer to court. In 2010 the Labour Court ruled in her favour, but the South African Police Service (SAPS) appealed the judgment. In November

2012, five years after the original posting, the Labour Appeal Court announced its judgment, ruling in favour of the SAPS.

In June 2014, Barnard resigned from the police force after more than twenty-five years of service.

'In my heart I will always be a police officer. It truly was my life's calling, but there is no future for me there. They only look at the colour of your skin,' says Barnard, who was offered a job as a forensic investigator with First National Bank.

Solidarity, the main trade union for Afrikaners, claims that the entire affirmative action plan of the SAPS should be declared unconstitutional and invalid. They helped Barnard appeal to the Constitutional Court, but in September 2014 the court found the SAPS not to be guilty of discrimination.

'Something that wrong cannot be right. The only thing that stood between her and her dream was the colour of her skin. Barnard and the public are the losers in this case,' says Solidarity Chief Executive Dirk Hermann, who has filed a complaint against the South African government for violating the United Nations' declaration on the elimination of all forms of racial discrimination.

* * *

With the fall of apartheid, the new black leadership faced daunting social and economic challenges. Black people, historically barred from most professional positions, wanted rapid change. There was a sense that it was symbolically important for South Africans to see people of colour in positions classically held by white individuals in order to create a sense of possibility for black youth. In order to accelerate change, the ANC government chose to implement affirmative action legislation.

The term 'affirmative action' was first used in the United States in 1961, in a document signed by President John F. Kennedy. In 1965, following his appointment to office two years prior,

AFFIRMATIVE ACTION

President Lyndon B. Johnson introduced affirmative action as a temporary policy to redress the racial imbalances that remained in spite of constitutional guarantees and laws banning discrimination. The idea was to ensure that black Americans and other minorities enjoyed the same opportunities for school admissions, career advancement and salary increases as white Americans did.

In South Africa, the intention was the same. The new government felt that, even with a new constitution, the competition for jobs was prejudiced against historically or previously disadvantaged individuals who, because of apartheid, lacked the educational background, experience or skills of their white counterparts. And unless they were provided with access to the means and resources with which to overcome their past marginalisation, the patterns of economic control, ownership and management produced by the apartheid system would remain unchanged.[4]

In 1998, the government passed the Employment Equity Act obliging employers of fifty or more workers, or companies with an annual turnover greater than the determined threshold per industry, to draft and implement plans aimed at making their workforce demographically representative at all levels: that is, roughly 75 per cent black, 52 per cent female and 5 per cent disabled. Companies had to report their progress annually to the Department of Labour.[5]

At first the ANC measured the success of transformation by how fast white civil servants in senior positions could be pushed out. Between 1994 and 1999, the share of white civil servants fell from 44 per cent to 18 per cent of all positions. Between 1998 and 2002, approximately 117,000 white civil servants, most of them Afrikaners, left their jobs. By 2002, heavy fines were introduced for medium and large companies that failed to reach their affirmative action targets. Companies rushed to replace as many senior white staff as quickly as possible and those who had been laid off, or were newly graduated, struggled to find employment.[6]

But, oddly enough, in some ways this actually benefitted many Afrikaners. The new legislation pushed many out of the public sector and into the private sector. Instead of being government officials they were more or less forced into entrepreneurship. As a result, many ended up making more money. In 1994, 75 per cent of white people earning more than 500,000 rand per year were formally employed. By 2009, 75 per cent of the white people in this income bracket were self-employed.[7]

But it wasn't enough for the government to focus on labour. Ownership, too, became an important measure of transformation. Noting that most companies were still controlled by white individuals, in 2003 the government introduced the Broad-Based Black Economic Empowerment Act, commonly known as BEE. In the legislative context 'black' was a generic term that included Coloured and Indian people.

While affirmative action only applied to companies with fifty employees or more, BEE legislation applied to all organisations with an annual turnover of more than five million rand. In a relatively complex scoring system, companies were rated on how well they adhered to the rules governing BEE, which required a certain percentage of ownership, management and control of any company to be in black hands.

On the surface, the case for affirmative action seemed obvious. In the past, white people, no matter how lazy or stupid, were pretty much guaranteed a job, while black people, no matter how smart or motivated, were barred from most opportunities. For example, during apartheid there was only one black employee at Koeberg, South Africa's high-security nuclear power plant. His job was to run away from the guard dogs, to train them to bite black trespassers.[8]

The fact that black South Africans were now free to compete would change nothing. Education, skills and experience had to be built up over time.

AFFIRMATIVE ACTION

Many argue that affirmative action, though right in principle, has been taken too far and that it is not achieving the intended results. One such person is Paul Joubert, a senior researcher at Solidarity.

'The law basically says that if you have two people you can employ with equivalent skills and one is black and the other is white, then you have to pick the black guy. That makes sense. There were inequalities in the past and we need to correct that. The affirmative action legislation is not too bad in the way it is crafted, it's the way it is implemented that is the problem,' says Joubert.

As a trade union, Solidarity focuses not only on workers' rights, but also on defending civil rights for its members. During the past few years, membership has increased dramatically as existing legislation regarding affirmative action and BEE is being implemented in increasingly controversial ways.

In 2005, Minister of Sport and Recreation Makhenkesi Stofile tried to apply affirmative action to the white-dominated sports of rugby and cricket, asking the predominantly Afrikaans rugby community and the largely English cricket community to 'sacrifice winning in the name of transformation'. His argument was that if a white sports team won, South Africa still lost.[9] [10] The initiative was successfully resisted, but the point was made.

Solidarity claims to have taken more than thirty affirmative action cases all the way to the Constitutional Court, and to have won about half of them, thus far.

'Officially, they can't fire you based on race, but often they will try to find an excuse in order to correct their demographic distribution and get higher scores. During the financial crisis of 2008, many companies tried to clear out their white employees in order to meet their employment equity targets. When companies downsize they are supposed to follow the principle of "last in, first out", but many companies let people go in a way that increased their employment equity. The government won't object to such treatment, so we have to,' says Joubert.

Sometimes a white applicant can get temporary work in a vacant position; that way, according to Joubert, he or she can be replaced as soon as a suitable black candidate comes along. In 2007 more than 40 per cent of the technical positions at municipalities were vacant at any one time.[11]

The economically active part of the population is 12 per cent white. If companies have more than 12 per cent white employees their BEE score goes down, which in turn affects their ability to bid on government contracts and tenders. But according to Joubert, it doesn't go both ways:

'If a company has 15 per cent white employees it's a big problem, but if a company has 100 per cent black employees it's not a problem.'

Working with the government is practically impossible for companies who ignore BEE guidelines. But even for companies who aren't hoping for government contracts, the legislation still matters.

As Joubert explains: 'If I'm a construction company, the steel I buy for my business has to come from a company that has good scores on BEE, otherwise their low score will pull down the score of my company as well. It's known as the cascading effect.'

Calculating a company's BEE score is an extremely complicated and time-consuming process. Advising companies on the ins and outs of the law, and where they can find loopholes, has become an industry in itself.

'If you're starting a company, why should you be forced to bring in someone who didn't have the idea in the first place? It makes no sense to add people who don't create value. It is counterproductive and an infringement on the rights of free association,' says Joubert.

It has also been argued that BEE has actually had an adverse effect on black entrepreneurship, encouraging passivity among black youths who expect to be handed opportunities without putting in any significant effort. Consequently, competition among companies for well-educated and experienced black professionals is fierce. For example, after the Employment Equity Act was passed, Barloworld, a large industrial firm, began to offer newly qualified black accountants roughly twenty per cent more money than their white colleagues. In addition to this, they received an entry-level BMW and greater prospects for promotion. Even so, 'after a few months, they are mercilessly head-hunted,' Tony Phillips, then chief executive at Barloworld, told *The Economist*.[12]

If affirmative action policies are implemented without the support of policies designed to improve access to education, there is a real risk that the Employment Equity Act will simply empower a black elite and further entrench growing class inequalities in South Africa.[13] But while affirmative action also applies to university admissions, and thus functions as an attempt to solve this challenge, it also feeds racial tensions in the generation born after apartheid.

Many universities, such as the University of Cape Town, have implemented policies that favour black applicants. This causes many white students, most of whom were born after the fall of apartheid, to feel discriminated against.

'You can't just use race as a qualifier. Solidarity is right in saying that the policies create resentment among whites in a generation that has the potential for being non-racial in their thinking. But then the fact that Solidarity is complaining about these things in turn creates resentment in the black community where whites are regarded as being very privileged still,' says Lucy Holborn of the South African Institute of Race Relations.

She believes there are other ways of drafting policy that would generate similar results but without the stigma of racial discrimination. For instance, evaluating students based on socio-economic background instead of race would generate more or less the same outcome without inciting racial resentment.

Holborn tells me that even black people are starting to become critical of so-called positive discrimination.

'Many complain that people will always suspect they got something just because they are black and not because they were the best suited. Young blacks want to be judged on merit. So it's not just Solidarity complaining about these things, but also blacks who feel it perpetuates the idea that blacks aren't as capable,' she says.

She also feels that the implementation of the employment equity policies could have benefited from a bit more patience and better planning.

'We have been hugely increasing the number of black graduates in areas where there is a critical need of skills. But they are the first generation and they have only just graduated. Sometimes they get promoted to senior positions too fast,' she tells me.

Founded on a platform of non-racialism the ANC doesn't seem to see the inherent contradiction in using race-based affirmative action and economic empowerment policies to achieve transformation. Race is now used to promote the previously disadvantaged and disadvantage the previously advantaged, which means that your race still largely determines your opportunities in life. During apartheid it was common among Coloured people to try to pass as white in order to have access to better education, jobs and promotions. With the affirmative action legislation, the same phenomenon can be observed in reverse, with people now trying to pass as black. One example is the Chinese population of South Africa. During apartheid, most Chinese were classified either as Coloured or white. As a result they were at first excluded as beneficiaries of the new black empowerment legislation. However, in 2008, Chinese people were reclassified as black after the Chinese Association of South Africa took the South African government to court and won.[14]

AFFIRMATIVE ACTION

The previously disadvantaged include all non-whites, women and the disabled. This means that close to ninety-five per cent of the population, with black people at the top, are entitled to preferential treatment in hiring, promotion, university admissions and the award of government contracts. The flipside of this is that if you are a white male, and hence part of the five per cent considered the most 'previously advantaged', your chances of being accepted to university, finding a job or being promoted, are that much slimmer. As a result, many have ended up leaving the country. Estimates vary, but according to Alana Bailey, Deputy Chief Executive of AfriForum, about one million people emigrated from South Africa between 1994 and 2006. A great many of these emigrants were white Afrikaners.

'We didn't just lose one generation, but all of their descendants. With affirmative action, people felt there was no viable career facing them. The people who left were the best educated ones, the type of people we need here,' she says.

According to Bailey, even among those who have stayed in South Africa, many have 'emigrated into themselves': 'People have withdrawn from civil society to take care of themselves and their family and that is where their commitment ends.'

AfriForum organises campaigns to try to persuade Afrikaners in exile to return home.

'Until 2007, the main reason that people stayed in exile was employment, but then it changed to crime. Now people say they won't come back because they are scared. They want to live without having to look over their shoulder; they want to bring up their children somewhere safe. Other growing reasons include the deterioration of service delivery and the collapse of the educational system,' says Bailey.

She believes that emigration has been adversely affected by the global financial crisis, but is convinced that there will be a new wave of emigrants as soon as the economy abroad picks up.

22

THE BROEDERBOND

BETRAYED AND REBORN

In a poorly lit room lies a bundle, wrapped in a sheet and fixed by a dagger. Across it, blood-red letters spell out the word VERRAAD—treason. The candles flicker from the sudden gust of wind when a brother steps up and swiftly drives his dagger deep into the bundle. Behind him the others wait their turn. One by one they walk up to stab the dummy, in a symbolic demonstration of the penalty for betrayal. Meanwhile, a solemn voice intones: 'He who betrays the Bond will be destroyed by the Bond. The Bond never forgets. Its vengeance is swift and sure. Never yet has a traitor escaped his just punishment.'[1]

While, over time, the induction ceremonies of the Broederbond became less ritualistic, the oath to take its secrets to the grave remained. Given the number of members and how long the organisation existed for, there were surprisingly few leaks. But when they did happen, it was regarded as extremely serious.

Beyers Naudé was the first Broeder to betray the organisation. He was the son of Reverend Jozua Naudé, the minister who gave spiritual guidance to the three young men who first formed the

Broederbond in 1918, and considered by many to have been a co-founder. As such, Beyers Naudé soon rose to become a prominent member. But in the 1960s he had a change of heart about apartheid—influenced partly by the Sharpeville Massacre. He gave some Broederbond documents to a fellow theologian outside of the organisation, Professor Albert Geyser, for advice on whether he should leave the Bond. Geyser gave the documents to the *Sunday Times* who published them. As a consequence, the newspaper was raided and the documents seized. The journalist who wrote the story had his car sabotaged and received offers of bribes for giving up his source. And later on, the minister at the local church refused to baptise his daughter.[2]

As for Naudé, a minister like his father, he was forced to resign from his congregation in Northcliff and stripped of his status as a pastor. He also received death threats. In 1973, his passport was withdrawn, and in 1977 he was declared a banned person with severe restrictions on his movements. He was also forbidden to be in a room with more than one person at a time. While he inspired other Afrikaner dissidents, the mainstream Afrikaner community ostracised him until the very end of apartheid.

In 1994, the Broederbond transformed itself into an organisation open to any Christian, Afrikaans-speaking individual who considers themselves to be an Afrikaner. It changed its name to the Afrikanerbond, but kept the old headquarters in Auckland Park, Johannesburg. In post-apartheid South Africa, without its network of strategically positioned members, its influence quickly faded. With a dwindling membership, the organisation was forced to relocate to far smaller facilities.

* * *

'189 Beyers Naudé Drive, please.' I smile as I announce my destination to the taxi driver.

Through an ironic twist of fate, the new offices of the Afrikanerbond are situated on the street named after their first traitor. I find them on the third floor of a rundown building, hidden among many other small and obscure organisations.

An older lady greets me in Afrikaans—she is sporting a hairstyle of artificial curls that was last popular in the 1950s. I tell her I've come to see Chief Secretary Jan Bosman. She leads me down a corridor. We pass a small room where another elderly woman sits at her desk surrounded by file cabinets. She is thinner and fragile-looking, wearing a similar short, curled hairstyle, and a knitted cardigan. Her posture is slack and her shoulders slope forward as though she spends her days carrying the full weight of the contents of the tall grey cabinets. Our eyes meet as I walk past and something about her gaze reminds me of a caged animal at a mismanaged zoo: trapped, a little anxious, but above all resigned.

Only four employees remain at the Bond—human relics of a long-ago era. Even the chief secretary, Jan Bosman, is a lot older than I expected after having spoken to him on the phone. He is in his fifties, double-chinned and of a pinkish complexion; a knitted blue vest is pulled tightly over his bulging belly.

'There is no secrecy anymore. No things going on in dark rooms as in the past,' he tells me; and, as if to prove a point, he leaves me alone among the file cabinets while he goes to fetch coffee.

Bosman started his career in the National Party as part of De Klerk's election team, where he was responsible for media relations. He later worked for the Democratic Alliance (DA) and eventually joined provincial government in Western Cape where he worked for six years until 2007 when he became Chief Secretary of the Bond. At the Afrikanerbond he feels he can combine his interest in politics with his interest in Afrikaner culture.

Both Bosman's father and grandfather were members of the original Broederbond, and Bosman himself was active in the organisation's junior wing—the Ruiterwag.

'Like most youth organisations we were a bit more progressive, but membership and activities were still confidential,' says Bosman.

The extreme secrecy that characterised the Bond in those days is illustrated by the fact that the organisation's affairs could not even be discussed between husband and wife, nor between father and son—even if the son belonged to the Ruiterwag.

'There was a custodian who gave the youth members information about what was going on in the mother organisation and vice versa. But information was limited,' Bosman tells me. 'My father and grandfather never told me anything about their activities, but in speaking with them afterwards I have understood that we shared much of the same experiences only ours was at the university level while theirs was at a broader community level. We shared the same anxieties and faced the same problems.'

As a member of the Ruiterwag, Bosman tried to influence the students towards certain decisions. He also tried to get members of the NP elected to student positions. 'Political affiliation was very important at that stage,' he says.

The aims and objectives of the Ruiterwag were the same as those of the parent body. Membership also followed the same exclusive pattern and was by invitation only. Men between the ages of eighteen and twenty-eight who were outstanding members of the Christian Afrikaner community could be recommended for membership according to the same principles as the Broederbond. They then had to swear a solemn oath 'to serve God and your people faithfully to the death without expecting honour or reward.'[3]

Bosman still believes each member was driven by a sincere will to bring about change and a better society.

'So why was there a need to be so secretive?' I ask.

'We belonged to an exclusive group of people who got first-hand information about what was happening on a constitutional or parliamentary level. It made you feel special to have access to information about what was going to happen beforehand. We could have open discussions and tackle certain aspects that worried us. For example, concerning the Group Areas Act there were those who felt it was still needed while others were vehemently opposed it. You could speak freely whatever your opinion safe in the knowledge that when you left that room it wouldn't be held against you. In political parties you don't have that liberty.'

Bosman believes that, in 1986, when the Broederbond issued their document containing recommendations for a more open society, 80 per cent of Afrikaners weren't ready.

'We influenced them a lot. We had to for our own survival, but as a result many Afrikaners blame us for what is now happening in the country,' he says.

After issuing the document, the Broederbond lost about a third of its members, according to Pieter de Lange, the Bond's chairman at the time. After the end of apartheid, many others followed, fearing repercussion.

'Between 1994 and 1997, we lost a lot of people from the civil service, the academy, army and police who feared a witch-hunt,' says Bosman.

On the wall of Bosman's office hangs a framed copy of The Vow made at Blood River. He says it acts as a reminder of his heritage and responsibilities. In the adjacent conference room is a framed copy of the Afrikanerbond's code of conduct—the same ethical guidelines used by the Broederbond in the old days. I read the list: 'To serve, not be served'; 'To give, not receive.' Many of the old goals also remain. Just like the Broederbond, the organisation's modern incarnation works to promote Afrikaner interests, particularly the language and culture of Afrikaners. This core issue is shared with many similar organisations who believe there is a serious threat to the Afrikaans language and, particularly, Afrikaans-medium education. The organisation also shares the common Afrikaner grievances of affirmative action, Black Economic Empowerment (BEE) and cadre deployment (meaning either that you have to be an ANC member to get a job, or that the ANC will decide where you will be appointed). A lot of effort is also spent interpreting the constitution and explaining to Afrikaners how best to claim the minority rights listed therein.

'The constitution says "unity through diversity", but all the focus is on unity and none of it on diversity. The country is becoming Anglicised,' Bosman claims.

The main difference between the old Broederbond and the new Afrikanerbond is that the current organisation focuses on the Afrikaner community as part of a bigger group of minorities in South Africa and claims to work on behalf of all these minorities.

'There is a lot of self-centeredness,' says Bosman. 'Many Afrikaners seem to believe they are the only ones with problems; that only they are the victims of murder and crime. That is not true. We have to address South Africa's problems, not only Afrikaner problems. The division is not between black and white. Black and white each consist of many subgroups. There is a responsibility on our side to also help other minority groups. As Afrikaners we want to work towards a better South Africa.'

Many black Africans have huge respect for what the Broederbond did for the Afrikaner. Pieter de Lange, chairman of the Broederbond between 1983 and 1993, says that he was even approached by some Frelimo leaders in Mozambique asking for advice on how to do for their people what the Broederbond had done for Afrikaners in South Africa. In 2007, Fikile Mbalula, then president of the ANC Youth League and current minister of sport and recreation, said that South Africa 'needed a black Broederbond' to correct the injustices of the past. The desire for economic liberation among black South Africans, their frustration of feeling like second-class citizens in the land of their birth, of doing all the work while someone else collects the profit, are almost perfect echoes of the Afrikaner grievances and demands that first gave rise to the Broederbond. Even the strategies implemented by the Afrikaners to resolve their challenges are to a large extent being copied by the black South African elite. The ANC's policy of BEE and the widespread nepotism within the party are not all that different from the Broederbond's old strategies of how to favour and enrich their own people.[4]

Like the original Broederbond, the Afrikanerbond is largely a lobby organisation, identifying problems or threats to the Afrikaner that it then sets out to resolve through discussion, debate and campaigns of influence.

'We are solution-oriented, but the government is not very willing to listen anymore,' Bosman tells me.

The reason is obvious. While Bosman claims that the organisation still has members in cabinet and parliament, even within the ANC, they are obviously not as strong as they used to be, and so the ability to influence government has drastically declined.

According to Bosman, even among mainstream Afrikaners a great deal of scepticism remains: 'There is still a widespread distrust in the community for what we do. Many were highly critical of the secrecy. But I'm sure some of that also comes from the fact that they weren't invited to become members. They called it an organisation for career advancement. When people claimed they couldn't be promoted or appointed to certain positions because they weren't members of the Broederbond, it was not true. We did not make leaders of members, we made members of leaders. Only people who had already proven themselves as leaders were recruited to the organisation,' he says.

Bosman claims that is still the recruitment policy today.

The organisation's new logo is a triangle inside a circle. Bosman tells me the triangle symbolises the dependence on God and the interrelated strength between men; the surrounding circle symbolises unity; and the legs of the triangle symbolise community, fraternity and transparency.

But despite continuous claims of being an open, transparent organisation, membership lists are still secret, as are the organisation's meetings. The aims and goals of the organisation are public, as well as any documents they publish—but little else.

'Things like board meetings are confidential at any company. You don't talk about what is being said there,' Bosman argues.

He estimates the membership for 2013 at around 4,000 members, but he is unable to tell me their demographic make-up.

'It is still predominately an organisation consisting of white male Afrikaners,' is all he says.

'But are there some Coloured members?' I ask.

'Yes, in the Western Cape.'

'Are we talking one per cent or ten per cent? Is it a few individuals or a larger group?' I press.

'A few individuals.'

'And what is their perception of the organisation?'

'That we are still a white, male-dominated organisation.'

23

TERRENCE PELSER WILL NEVER FLY

Corné carefully places the meat on the braai, steps back, and cracks open a beer. Bare-chested and fit; he wears only shorts and flip-flops. On his head rests a cowboy hat and on his belt sits a matching Texas buckle, both presents from his brother, a civil engineer living in Texas. A long, thick scar stretches vertically up his tanned, muscular belly.

'I swallowed a big coin when I was a kid and had to have surgery,' he says when I ask.

'You should have said you were attacked by a lion or something cool like that,' I comment.

'Ja. When I was younger I used to say a Kaffir sliced me open with a panga. Everyone believed me ... But I'm done lying now.'

For those Oranians who can't or won't submit to the 'no drugs, no alcohol' policy, there is no room at C-block. One afternoon at the community pool, I meet two such fellows, Corné and Terrence, who have come to enjoy a braai. Corné was recently evicted for violating the no-drinking policy and has just finished moving his belongings to his new home—a rented room on the other side of town.

Corné is twenty-eight years old. He moved to Orania from Pretoria three months ago, after being unable to find work 'on the outside'.

'Do you like it here?' I ask him.

'Ja, but *man*, it's hard work!' He extends his hands for me to see the calluses on the pads of his fingers.

Corné works long hours, six days a week. The sixth day he works for free. The idea is that if he works twenty Saturdays in a year, at the end of the year he gets one month's extra salary. He refers to it as a bonus. Others more economically savvy call it forced savings or a way for management to retain their workforce until year-end.

Terrence, twenty-one, is also from Pretoria. His eyes are red; he appears to have been smoking something other than tobacco. He doesn't say much, just smiles awkwardly when spoken to, whether by Corné or myself. It's Saturday evening and the sun is beginning to set on their braai. I ask what people do here for fun. At first they laugh and shake their heads, as if to imply that in Orania there is no such thing, but after a while it turns out there is in fact a pub called *Ommi Draai*, and the young men offer to take me there.

Having someone to escort me turns out to be a good thing, as there is no way I would have found the place on my own. Stacked away in an unpaved alley behind the grocery store, it is, quite literally, a hole in the wall.

The owner is eighteen-year-old Wayne Wolsen. One week before his birthday he bought the place for 100,000 rand. Only the lady who sold it to him didn't really own it. She took off with all the money and he had to purchase the place again from its rightful owner. This time for 80,000 rand. Wayne lost his leg in a car accident due to mistreatment by the paramedics. His family sued, and Wayne received some money, which he used to buy the local pub (twice), a house in Orania and a car. But now the pub is up for sale as Wayne is heading to Cape Town to study to become a paramedic himself. He wants to do his part to prevent what happened to him from happening to others.

Wayne sets me up with the evening's first round of drinks and I return to the table where Corné and Terrence wait thirstily. Over the course of the evening, Corné's story emerges bit by bit. And it's not pretty. His mom was a crack cocaine addict. Corné started using drugs at the age of six when he stumbled across his mom's stash. From there, life was a series of downward spirals.

My eyes are drawn to his lower arms, which are lined with scars. He follows my gaze.

'Ja, looks bad. It's from the rage. The *rage*, man.'

I look at him quizzically.

'When the rage comes I just get this feeling ... and I start cutting myself. With glass.'

Corné's face tenses up and he gestures violently at his arms as though he's attacking himself right there.

'My stepmom was abusive. She started abusing me when I was six.'

He doesn't elaborate on what she did, what type of abuse he means, and I can't bring myself to ask. He's too agitated and there's something desperate about him, a darker spirit that I didn't notice at the pool. Maybe it's the alcohol that brings it out, or maybe it's the subject matter.

'And, I don't know ... I just started to cut myself. I'm a little better now. Only happens when I get too drunk. I'll smash a bottle and cut myself up.'

A few years ago, things were looking up for Corné. He found love and was about to start a family, but then something went horribly wrong. When his girlfriend was seven months pregnant she overdosed, killing herself and the baby.

'She got spooked. Didn't think she had what it takes to be a mother,' Corné says.

Devastated, Corné hung himself, but his brother pulled him down and managed to resuscitate him. Ever since, life has just been one long battle for survival.

He tells me that he tries his best to have faith in the Lord: 'Prayer works, you know. One time my dog got really sick and I was sure I was going to lose him, so I prayed and prayed. I told the Lord I couldn't handle having anything else taken from me. And it worked!' His wide contagious smile rips across his face. 'Against all odds my dog recovered!'

Corné's most treasured possession is an eighteenth-century King James Bible.

'You know my favourite part?' he says, leaning forward across the table.

Like a pastor building up to the crescendo of his sermon, his eyes are wild with excitement, his finger pointing, as if down from the heavens, into my chest. He emphasises each word: 'It says: "I—have—great—things—in—store—for—you".'

He stares at me in blessed illumination, then collapses back into his chair and grabs his beer. 'That's my favourite part,' he says, and takes a gulp.

While Corné tells his story, Terrence sits quietly drinking his beer. He keeps up a much higher drinking pace than the rest of us. Then Corné is challenged to a game of pool and Terrence and I are left alone at the table. Still, he doesn't speak. His English is not great, my Afrikaans worse, and with the music blasting from the speakers I give up after a few feeble attempts at having a conversation. It's like his whole being exudes pain, but he can't or won't tell his story.

Once Corné has returned, Terrence finally leans across the table and mumbles something in my direction. I still can't understand him, but Corné has heard.

'He wants to know if you came here by plane,' says Corné.

'Yes, Sweden is a long way away,' I reply.

'What is it like?' asks Terrence, this time loud and clear enough for me to hear.

He tilts his head back and looks at the ceiling.

'Up there,' he adds.

'Above the clouds?' I ask.

He nods.

'It's nice,' I say, and immediately regret my bland description.

But he seems satisfied. He nods again and smiles, seemingly pleased. I appear to have confirmed his suspicions that it's better 'up there'.

We sit in silence for a while. Then I ask:

'Do you have a dream, Terrence?'

He shakes his head.

'If you could have anything you wanted, anything at all, what would it be?' I insist.

'A house with a view,' he finally replies.

'A view of what?'

'Of the sea.'

'And what would you want to do for a living?'

He looks up towards the sky again.

'Be one of those guys.'

'A pilot?' I ask.

He nods.

And that's where it ends. That's all I get out of Terrence: silence and an unattainable dream. He is young and he has plenty of time to pull his life together and make something of himself. But somehow I know—without quite being able to explain how—Terrence Pelser will never fly.

16 DECEMBER 2006

A NAME-CALLING FIGHT

As the ten-year anniversary of democracy approached, the South African government decided to build Freedom Park, a heritage destination and alternative memorial park, across the road from the Voortrekker Monument in Pretoria. The sprawling lush area with its mirror pond and architecturally innovative monuments provides a stark contrast to the monolithic 1930s granite construction of the Voortrekker Monument.

On 16 December 2006, Thabo Mbeki hosted a commemoration at Freedom Park celebrating the completion of the second phase of construction, which included the erection of a 697-metre-long wall of names honouring the heroes who died in the struggle for freedom.[1] A year later the park opened its doors to the public, but construction was still ongoing. In 2011, the government spent 50 million rand to maintain the park and an additional 200 million on further construction.[2]

But it's not just large-scale memorials and museums that are competing with one another. South Africa is literally in the midst of a name war. In 2012, the name of the road that runs past the Voortrekker Monument—Voortrekker Road—was changed to Steve Biko. Hundreds of other streets across South Africa have also undergone name changes and countless others are currently in debate.

The old names remain for a period of six months, but with a red line through them so that people can find their way around, until they either learn the new names or the map books are updated. Long streets are frequently divided up into multiple segments with different names.

'There is enough new development to give new names to buildings and streets without having to change all the old ones,' says Cecilia Kruger of the Heritage Foundation, which manages the Blood River Site and the Voortrekker Monument in Pretoria.

A street around the corner from her house is being renamed from Louis Botha to January Masilela.

'Botha died in 1919. He was the first prime minister of South Africa and has nothing to do with apartheid. Nobody knows who this January Masilela was. They should at least publish something in the papers to let people know who he was,' she says.

Whole provinces and towns are also being renamed. Between 2000 and 2010, 916 geographic and place names in South Africa were changed. The list included the names of 38 towns, 72 rivers, 13 mountains, 16 dams and 2 airports.[3]

The city of Pietersburg has become Polokwane, Potgietersrust is now called Mokopane, and since 2005 there has been an on-and-off debate about whether or not the country's executive capital, Pretoria, should be renamed Tshwane. A first step in this direction was taken in 2000 with the creation of Tshwane as a larger metropolitan municipality to include Pretoria and neighbouring towns. In 2011, the mayor stated that Pretoria itself would be renamed Tshwane by the end of 2012. By 2015, the name change had still not been effected, nor the matter dismissed.

The battle over the naming of Louis Trichardt, a small town situated at the foot of the Soutpansberg mountain range near the border with Zimbabwe, is an illustrative example of an on-going name battle. Founded in 1899, the town was named after Voortrekker leader Louis Johannes Tregardt. After the fall of apartheid, the new local government wanted to change the town's name to Makhado, after a nineteenth-century VhaVenda king, who courageously opposed the Boers until his death in 1897. But Makhado had already been approved as a name for another town in the area, so the South African Geographical Names Council denied the request.[4] The municipality then tried to persuade the existing Makhado to change its name to Dzanani, in order to free up the name Makhado for their use. But Dzanani had also already been approved for another town so the Names Council rejected the proposal in July 2000.

The subject was dropped until December 2002, when SABC News showed municipality employees erecting new signboards with the name Makhado. Three new names had been approved in the Limpopo province, media reported. Dzanani would now be called Mphephu so that Makhado could be called Dzanani, freeing up the name of Makhado for Louis Trichardt.[5]

The sudden name change upset not only the Afrikaner community, but other ethnic minorities as well, including the Tsonga people, among whom King Makhado was known as a violent oppressor.

In October 2005, the Louis Trichardt Chairpersons' Association, an alliance of fifty-one of the town's cultural and business organisations, fought the name change in the Pretoria High Court. They claimed that the inhabitants of the town had not been consulted. The Pretoria High Court dismissed their application in November 2005, but the group appealed.[6] In September 2005, a statue of King Makhado was unveiled, while a statue of Trichardt was removed and stored in a toolshed. After complaints, the statue of Louis Trichardt was moved to a public library, but the damage had been done. The Makhado statue was vandalized—painted in orange, white and blue, the colours of the old South African flag.[7]

In 2007, the Supreme Court of Appeal reversed the name change and the Limpopo town was once again called Louis Trichardt.

'God did not make a mistake to give us different cultural communities. Together we can build a rich future if we respect our history and guard over our cultural heritage,' said Councillor MP Nxumalo, member of the Shangaan Royal Council, at a celebration of the Supreme Court victory.

'With all the money that they waste on a one-sided name change effort, they can build their own new town, which they can call what they like,' he continued, advising municipal councillors to start working for the people instead of fighting for positions and money.[8]

But the municipal council had not yet given up. As soon as the Supreme Court announced its verdict, they vowed to file a new application and have the name changed back to Makhado.[9] In October 2011, they reached their goal when the Department of Arts and Culture announced the naming of Louis Trichardt back to Makhado. Within two weeks, several thousand signatures had been collected in protest of the name change.[10]

In October 2014, the North Gauteng High Court reversed the name changing, turning the town back to Louis Trichardt once again.[11] But two weeks after the ruling, the town's mayor, David Mutavhatsindi, said the municipal council had not yet been officially informed about the town's name reverting back to Louis Trichardt and that they planned to seek legal advice 'to check the validity of the settlement.'[12]

And so the battle continues.

For a country struggling with among the largest disparity between rich and poor in the world,[13] it says a great deal about the importance placed on history when naming and memorials take precedence over education and infrastructure in budget allocation.

Those in favour argue that name changes are an important form of symbolic reparation for human rights abuses and a mechanism of transitional justice. And the fact is that the Afrikaners did the same. After the Battle of Blood River, the Voortrekkers changed the names of places, mountains and rivers from Zulu to Afrikaans. In 1938 there was another massive wave of name changes as many streets were given Afrikaans names.

'It was an expensive lesson that South Africa obviously hasn't learnt,' says Kruger. 'Huge amounts of money are being spent on correcting the imbalances of the past instead of investing in the future.'

How to reframe the past in a way that satisfies those who were disempowered, while at the same time not offending those who disempowered them, remains a challenge. Some old monuments have been removed, like the statue of former Prime Minister Hendrik Verwoerd (relocated to Orania), but for the most part, they have been left untouched. This is not completely uncontroversial, as many ANC leaders still feel uncomfortable among these reminders of the past. For example, during the inauguration of President Mbeki in 1999, the statues of former leaders Louis Botha, Jan Smuts and J.B.M. Hertzog, as well as the huge bust of J.G. Strydom, were covered with cloth.[14]

'We have such an embattled past. We are so diverse. It's very easy to say that there's unity and diversity and all that wonderful rainbow nation stuff, but the truth is things aren't working out and the fact that everybody had such high hopes only makes it worse,' says Kruger.

24

CHESS WITH THE COLONEL

'The crime that is latent in us we must inflict on ourselves [...] Not on others.'

J.M. Coetzee, *Waiting for the Barbarians*

Honour is one of the most important values of any good soldier. A soldier hopes for victory, or, if that's not possible, at least for an honourable defeat. For many Afrikaners faced with the end of apartheid, there was neither. There was simply shame: the disgrace of having fought for an unjust cause, followed by the humiliation of being left to bear the guilt.

Fransie, fifty-one, was a colonel in the military intelligence bureau during apartheid. After twenty-three years of service, he now works as a gardener in Orania, clearing out stones from the little patch of dirt and grass outside the administrative offices on Main Street. He appears torn between the desire to tell me his story and maintaining a vow of secrecy that is presumably self-imposed.

I take a seat on a bench in the little garden and wait. A pattern soon emerges. The Colonel will rake the soil in silence for a few minutes, then stop and remain for a few seconds almost completely motionless in contemplation, before finally walking over to tell me something. A couple of sentences, never more, and then the raking resumes. It is clear he is not entirely sane. He seems to think he is being watched and whenever a car comes close or someone walks our way, he rushes back to his duties.

Fransie is unbearably thin, but strong—all sinew and muscle, devoid of fat. His back is slightly bent and his shoulders slumped, like a humbled boy who spends too much time looking at his shoes. His teeth are rotten and his eyes like shattered blue marbles. Every dawn and dusk he can be seen outside C-block doing frantic sit-ups, knee-bends and push-ups, before setting out on one of his long runs. He runs to keep in shape, and to keep one step ahead of his demons.

At first glance, the Colonel could easily be written off as a poor, dull, old man who has failed to make a decent living for himself despite all the privileges bestowed on him during apartheid. But looks are deceiving. The Colonel speaks four languages; easily slipping in and out of whichever one he is addressed in. He is a wonder of eloquence and I find myself wishing I had known him before he broke. In bits and pieces, tarnished fragments of brilliance, the story of his life emerges.

With Fransie there is no 'I was following orders' or 'I only did what I was told.' He takes full responsibility for his actions.

'Moral courage is a far scarcer commodity than physical courage. It comes with a high price tag,' he says.

Fransie always knew he was meant to be a soldier.

'I knew before I turned six—with the kind of clarity very few people ever have,' he tells me.

His father was also in the military and fought on Hitler's side in the Second World War: 'He didn't believe in the ideology but used the system for rapid promotion,' says Fransie. 'He regarded the early successes of Hitler as a road to personal advancement.'

Fransie's own military career followed a similar pattern to that of his father.

'I was never a patriot. I never believed in what I was doing and I didn't subscribe to the myths of racial superiority. It was just a game to me. And in that game a lot of people lost a great deal.' At this he pauses and looks down at his rake. His shoulders fall forward; his body deflates; he continues: 'It doesn't put me in a very good light, does it? But it's true ... Morally it makes you more culpable if you *don't* believe, than if you do.'

'But if you didn't believe, how could you do the things you did?' I ask.

His answer is immediate, it comes with the certainty of someone who has spent time reaching for an explanation: 'You compartmentalise. You don't involve your emotions. There were even certain things that I went ahead and did completely at my own initiative.'

One of the organisations Fransie worked to infiltrate was the End Conscription Campaign, an anti-apartheid organisation that opposed the conscription of all white South African men into the defence force.

'They were encouraging young people to not conduct their service, but also encouraging sabotage among those who were currently doing their service. I found an informant in this organisation, a student whose brother was serving time for desertion. We told him that if he helped us, in six months' time he would get his brother back. Otherwise he wouldn't see him again,' says Fransie.

The student provided Fransie and his crew with information and, when the six months were up, his brother was released. The student then wanted to stop working for them, as agreed.

'But by this point we had him on tape giving us information and accepting money. We told him he had to keep helping us. He had no choice.'

A while later the student gave Fransie information about a plan to blow up a draft station. The plan was stopped and the people involved arrested, including one of the student's closest friends. It turned out the friend had a heart condition. Allegedly, the stress of the interrogation caused him to collapse and die.

'My informant, the student, walked in front of a train when he found out,' says Fransie. His face betrays no emotion, but he pauses and looks at me as if waiting to be scolded.

Because he didn't believe in the ideology of apartheid, Fransie had no problems staying on in the military after its fall. He finally resigned in 2002, supposedly because he had little chance of promotion.

'I wasn't going to do any favours for the ruling party. The interests of the country and of the ruling party were hard to differentiate. Nepotism is expected in African cultures. People are expected to help out their less favoured relatives. People were posted to me who weren't able to do their jobs and I wouldn't have it,' he says.

'If you had the chance to relive your life, would you do it all again?' I ask.

'Absolutely!' he replies. 'I had a great deal of fun. My work was much like putting together a jigsaw puzzle. It required intuition and patience. Impatience is one of the fatal flaws in intelligence work.'

Yet, after leaving the military, something snapped. Before settling down in Orania, the Colonel spent a great deal of time tracking down the families of victims who died as a result of his actions. He asked forgiveness from black and white alike.

'And it was always granted me, from both sides. It's a liberating feeling, receiving forgiveness, but then again if you do not forgive, you poison yourself as well,' he says.

Trying to make peace with his past has turned the Colonel into a religious man, although he is the first to admit that it doesn't fit with his 'logic streak'.

'Still, somehow I know it to be true. There is a Jesus-shaped hole in every man's heart. We try to fill it with all sorts of things, but nothing else fits.'

'Do you regret what you've done?' I press.

'There's no guilt left, at least not that I know of. For me it was just a game and I was lucky that people paid me to play. But I believe in karma. Nothing remains unpunished. You get away with nothing in this life. Sometimes justice takes longer, but eventually the punishment comes.'

The Colonel puts down his rake and heads back to his home at C-block, to a room no bigger than a prison cell, where no alcohol or female visitors are allowed. Of his worldly possessions, all that remain are a chessboard and a pair of running shoes. With little else to look at, the eyes of any visitor are drawn to his walls, covered by posters with quotations. 'ARE YOU A VICTIM OR A VOLUNTEER?' reads one.

'It's to make people think, which isn't easy around here,' Fransie says. 'I find I don't have a lot in common with people, but if someone stops by for the odd game of chess they'll see my quotes and be forced to think.'

The Colonel speaks about chess in a way that echoes his account of his military career: 'Chess is stylised warfare. It's war on a board. And at the end of the day you can't blame anyone else. You stand or fall by your own preparation and efforts,' he says.

Then he grows quiet and we sit in silence for a while; he looks at the ground.

When he looks up at me again, he resumes: 'Things happen for a reason, to teach you important life lessons. The first time it's an easy lesson, but if you don't learn it, it will come again and this time the stakes will be higher; there will be more pain involved. Money never meant much to me, but certain things did: my library, my CD collection, my uniforms—all became too important. They became idols and I had to learn to let go.'

Now, Fransie wants to live simply and stress-free. Orania's management offered him courses to further his skills as a handy man, but he declined.

'I'm done with responsibility,' he tells me. 'I have no aspiration left. Whatever remains is merely a bonus.'

16 DECEMBER 2008

AFRIKANER REVIVALISM

In 2008, a third reenactment of the Great Trek took place. A group of Afrikaners travelled by ox wagon across South Africa, ending at Blood River for the 16 December commemorations.

General Opperman, then director of the Voortrekker Monument and manager of the Blood River Heritage Site, estimated that as many as 5,000 people attended the celebrations at the Voortrekker Monument, while some 3,000 visited Blood River, the highest number during his period as director.[1]

Something was happening. Afrikaners were congregating to revive their culture, their history and their language.

There was a time when South African identity was synonymous with Afrikaner identity. The military actions of the 1980s were carried out in the name of South Africa, but it was Afrikaners acting in the name of South Africa. They experienced no discord between their goals and those of the country, even though they represented just ten per cent of its people. They considered themselves the essential population of South Africa. The rest were peripheral.

When the impact of post-apartheid transformation became clear, many Afrikaners were dumbstruck. For years they remained paralysed by guilt as their history was rewritten, altered or simply erased. But a generation later, things have started to change.

'Developments in recent years have changed the Afrikaner's perception of South Africa in a way that cannot be reversed,' says Carel Boshoff.

Boshoff speaks of three recent events that have served as wake-up calls for many Afrikaners, spawning reactions as diverse as emigration, cultural revitalisation and support for Orania. The first significant event was the failure of Eskom, South Africa's national power utility.

Shortly after its establishment in 1923, Eskom ranked among the top seven power generators in the world. Institutions like Eskom, as well as power plants and coalmines, were used to empower poor whites. They became places where struggling Afrikaners were given a chance. They were symbols of engineering achievement and economic success and, as such, they were great sources of pride. But after apartheid ended, Eskom was also a great place to start implementing affirmative action.

'There are a lot of jobs that you can hand out without noticing an immediate difference. But there was no long-term thinking,' says Boshoff.

Eskom used to produce excess capacity—over thirty per cent more electricity than what was needed. By 2007, production and utilisation were equivalent. But by the end of 2007, South Africa began to experience widespread blackouts as supply fell below demand. At the beginning of 2008, the national grid was close to a total collapse. Electricity rationing became a reality as Eskom introduced rolling blackouts based on a rotating schedule.

While many industries were adversely affected by the blackouts, the mining sector was the worst hit, losing millions of rands in production after Eskom instructed them to shut down their operations and reduce consumption to a minimum—just sufficient to evacuate workers from the mines. Given South Africa's reliance on precious metals exports, both the country's GDP and the value of the rand took heavy blows when the mines failed to deliver. It was also the mining industry that was forced to shed the most jobs during the global economic crisis that set in shortly afterwards.[2]

'For weeks on end, there would be blackouts, clearly because of a lack of planning and capacity. It was alienating. The number of people that started leaving after the blackouts began was massive,' Boshoff tells me.

Many Afrikaners blame the collapse of Eskom on affirmative action. Eskom engineers, however, claim the blackouts had nothing to do with affirmative action but that the collapse was caused by years of underinvestment; that the new government inherited a flawed structure.

In the late 1990s, leaders and decision-makers, both in Eskom and in the government, predicted that Eskom would run out of power reserves by 2007 unless investment was made in new power generation. Still, the government consistently denied Eskom the funds to build new power stations. Small and medium black enterprises were favoured for coal supply tenders over larger, more established corporations. Their inexperience caused an unreliable and insufficient supply of coal. In 2007, President Thabo Mbeki admitted that the lack of investment had been a mistake and that the government had failed to heed Eskom's warnings, but he did not respond to allegations that the government's black empowerment strategy had also contributed to the crisis.

Regardless of the root cause, many Afrikaners interpreted the blackouts as a sign that their fears were coming true: the new government had run Eskom to the ground and hence proven themselves unworthy rulers, incapable of basic service delivery.

According to Boshoff, the second event to stir the Afrikaner community was the election of Jacob Zuma as president.

'Afrikaners thought it totally impossible that he could get elected. Up until the very last moment, regardless of what the polls said, they were in denial. But it happened,' says Boshoff.

Then, finally, there was the murder of right-wing leader Eugene Terre'Blanche.

While, according to Boshoff, Terre'Blanche had very limited support, when he was killed people saw the approach of something more sinister. 'He was a strong man and a public figure. The fact that he hadn't been a target proved that South Africa still had certain freedom. But now people realised that something had changed and that your relative prominence will not save you,' he says.

When I ask him how these events have changed perceptions of Orania, he replies: 'We've experienced the changes in terms of acceptance. In the beginning we were truly eccentric. We were viewed as strange and regarded with patience at best. We weren't necessarily laughed at in the face, but we were regarded as mad. Now that has changed dramatically.'

Boshoff recently went to Pretoria to raise funds for the purchase of more farmland adjacent to Orania. 'I had no trouble raising millions of rand. It was a lot easier than I thought it would be. The attitude has fundamentally changed,' he says.

Prominent Afrikaners, and organisations representing Afrikaners across the country, confirm this change in attitude. While only a fraction are ready or willing to leave their jobs and social networks behind to pack up and move to Orania, many people have stopped laughing. There seems to be a growing respect—even admiration—for what Orania is trying to accomplish.

Frans de Klerk, CEO of the Orania Company and the town's municipal manager, also claims to be noticing an increased acceptance and support for Orania.

'We planned Orania foreseeing how things would develop. Today it's easier to get support because the political realities have developed the way we predicted. We're starting to find common ground with the majority,' he says. 'A lack of responsibility in government is the underlying problem. Orania is a model for local development.'

Mandela and Zuma have both visited Orania. According to De Klerk it was easier to get Zuma to understand the idea behind the initiative than it was Mandela.

'In 1995 it was still early days and Mandela was going to build a Rainbow Nation where there would be no need to escape into a separate community. Zuma, on the other hand, identifies very strongly with Zulu culture and seems to better understand the desire of a people to remain a people and preserve their culture,' De Klerk explains.

25

THE BATTLE FOR HISTORY

'To live without a past is worse than to live without a future.'

Elie Wiesel

'My great grandmother was in a concentration camp during the Anglo-Boer war,' says Wynand Boshoff.

'When the war was over and she was released, everything had been burnt down and all the cattle killed. A black man who worked for her before the war had hidden a bag of mielies, a pocket of peach pips and a milk cow. All through the war, the worker preserved this. If he had been caught, he too could have been sent to a concentration camp. When the war was over, together they plowed the fields with a milk cow and planted the mielies and the peach trees again.'

In many Afrikaner families there are these types of stories that portray content, docile workers and the benevolent masters who treated them with paternalistic kindness. These stories were an important part of building and maintaining the myth of the peaceful and frictionless coexistence between master and servant.

Wynand Boshoff, brother of Carl Boshoff, is a history teacher—he is responsible for creating a version of history for South

African school children that is written from an Afrikaner perspective. The material, primarily aimed at grades four through nine, is meant as an alternative or complement to the government curriculum. Wynand Boshoff is particularly interested in the portrayal of South African history by different interest groups over time.

'The British imperial school is the oldest. Natives were portrayed as being so much better off if they were on the imperial side,' he tells me. 'As long as no minerals were discovered, that is. There was benevolent British involvement and malignant Boers trying their best to enslave the natives and treating them badly.'

Then there is the Afrikaner national history, focused on the quest for freedom from the long arm of Britain. The environment is portrayed as hostile, as are the people. And, finally, there is the history of the black struggle, where differences between ethnic groups, like the Zulu and the Xhosa, are downplayed in favour of a common struggle history.

'Then, in the second half of the twentieth century, the black radical and British versions of history merged. Both saw the Afrikaner as the main antagonist,' says Wynand.

About the current government history curriculum, he expresses dissatisfaction: 'I'm disappointed, but not because it is Afrikaner-unfriendly. I expected that. They have changed the perspective, but are still focusing on Europe. The topics covered are the same: the French revolution, the Russian revolution, etcetera, but the interpretations are hostile. They have reduced all of Western civilisation to slave owners and oppressors. It's inexcusable on their side when they had the opportunity to broaden something that had been limited in its focus.'

But Wynand recognises the Afrikaner portrayal of history was also flawed: 'Afrikaner narratives ignored black achievements, but the black side is not merely ignoring, but even vilifying Afrikaner achievements. If I was black and was referred to as a savage my blood would boil too, but they don't replace it with well-founded arguments. I don't subscribe to the idea of objective history, but you can be honest or dishonest. They try to say that some things never happened.'

* * *

In the apartheid era, history was very Afrikaner-centric and the heroic characteristics of the *volk* were drastically exaggerated.

'Especially in the forties, fifties, and sixties. The Voortrekkers were all ten feet tall,' smiles Fransjohan Pretorius, Professor of History at the University of Pretoria. 'Already in the 70s us historians were realising this and started to write different stories. But it took the general population until the 80s and 90s until they realised they had been deceived.'

And those historians who first started addressing taboo topics were frequently ostracised.

'I remember when Albert Grundlingh wrote about Afrikaner collaborators during the Anglo-Boer wars. People didn't want to hear about that,' says Pretorius.

With a cultural identity that was largely a construct based on a skewed perception of history, finding out the truth about the past was an unpleasant wake-up call for many. For example, many Afrikaners weren't aware of the black concentration camps during the Second Anglo-Boer War.

'It wasn't part of the Afrikaner paradigm,' says Pretorius, who only found out about these concentration camps when in the Netherlands, where he attended university for three years in the early seventies.

Pretorius was in the library one day when he came across two fellow students. He asked them what they were working on and they said they were writing a paper about black involvement in the Anglo-Boer wars.

'But there were no blacks involved,' Pretorius replied.

The students then showed him photos from black camps in the very book they were reading. Pretorius was taken aback and says that experience taught him the importance of balance.

'I felt tricked, because it had been done on purpose. Just as the struggle history of today is purposefully partial. Now in the history books they write about the black and white camps, but only about the black suffering. The pendulum has swung to the other side where white suffering is completely ignored. We want to have it swing back to the middle,' he says.

After 1994, a new history syllabus was drafted, which came into operation in the late 1990s.

'After that, the black struggle history became *the* history,' says Pretorius. 'And, in the process, the history of the Afrikaner was absolutely put aside. Instead of merging the two, the one simply replaced the other.'

In 2005 he was asked to review a school history series, written by the Truth and Reconciliation Commission.

'The editor stated that they wanted an inclusive history, but that is not what it turned out to be, it turned out to be the struggle history all over,' he says.

Like many Afrikaners, Pretorius feels that the new government is committing many of the same mistakes as the apartheid regime did.

'What happened after 1948 is happening again now, with these historians rewriting history with a lot of emotion. Their ideology has triumphed and therefore they do not come up with a balanced portrayal,' he argues.

Pretorius believes that Afrikaners want to teach their children a different past: 'Many have bought in to the new South Africa, but also feel that their point of view should be acknowledged. They are not happy with the new syllabus.'

So Pretorius got together with sixteen other historians, most of them Afrikaners, but a few of them of British descent, to write a new version of history. Now, six years later, *Geskiedenis van Suid-Afrika: Van voortye tot vandag* is finally completed.

'We came up with what we regard as an attempt at a balanced history. It's hard because you tend to either emphasise something too much, or you ignore it. But this book includes the Afrikaner struggle as well as the black struggle,' says Pretorius.

'There is no attempt at vengeance. We try to understand rather than defend the past. There is a lot of vengeance in what today's historians say, and do, and write.'

But Pretorius is not hopeful about seeing the book accepted as part of the mainstream syllabus; the idea is that Afrikaner families can use it as a supplementary book.

Pretorius claims his book incorporates all perspectives. But when I ask him about the different black perspectives that exist, it soon becomes clear that *all* perspectives means the Afrikaner and the British, with non-white people lumped into one category despite the many different ethnic groups and nine official languages (besides English and Afrikaans).

'No, we haven't considered different black ethnic groups. That would make it too complicated, the book would be over a thousand pages,' Pretorius says when I ask.

The book will only be published in Afrikaans, unless there is enough public demand for an English translation.[1] But Pretorius translates the titles of the twenty-nine chapters for me. While there are three chapters devoted to Afrikaner nationalism, as well as one chapter explaining the reasons behind the Great Trek, and a more detailed one about the Great Trek itself, there is only one chapter devoted to 'black political awakening'. Only about thirty out of over six-hundred pages are devoted to South Africa after apartheid and what is referred to as the 'puberty' of South African democracy. Pretorius acknowledges that liberal British historians have been right in pointing out that history didn't start in 1652 with the Dutch arrival at the

Cape. He proudly announces that in his book this past mistake has been corrected.

'In this book we start with creation of the universe and how it happened that in this area there were diamonds and gold,' he informs me.

But after one short chapter entitled 'South Africa's early past' comes the chapter 'The Dutch at the Cape'.

'This still seems pretty Afrikaner-centric to me,' I comment.

'Well, you have to remember that most of the chapters are about the twentieth century, which is when the Afrikaner was very dominant.'

Pretorius seems genuine in his belief that he strove for and achieved balance. 'This is an attempt at reconciliation. We want to reconcile. We have an individual and a shared past. Let's take note of that. Your heroes might not be my heroes, but I respect your heroes,' he says.

Pretorius hopes that his book can broaden people's horizons.

'The struggle history is not bringing reconciliation. The history must be inclusive. We've achieved something if an Afrikaner reads about the black struggle and if a black person reads about the white concentration camps,' he says.

Afrikaners like Pretorius aren't the only ones who are critical of the current portrayal of the past. The Inkatha Freedom Party and its president, Mangosuthu Buthelezi, recently accused the ANC and President Jacob Zuma of 'rewriting' history and 'discrediting the role of the IFP in the liberation struggle'.[2]

As Buthelezi told the *Sunday Tribune* in May 2012: 'When I first read the ANC's concept document on the centenary, I warned my colleagues we were about to see the most profound rewrite of history imaginable.'[3]

I ask Professor Pretorius why he thinks there is so much focus on the past. He looks at me as though the answer is obvious, and replies: 'Everybody wants to justify his or her claim to the future of this country.'

26

THE *REAL* AFRICA

Maputo is a mere 455 km from Johannesburg, but Willem is right: it's a different world.

Willem is the journalist I met at the ANC Youth League demonstration; he is a young, modern South African who seems genuine in his desire to break out of the silos of racial segregation. So much so that he left South Africa to make a go of it in Mozambique.

As I make my way from the airport into town, I watch local life through the dirty windows of the taxi. Corrugated iron roofs simmer under the heat of the midday sun, turning the small concrete kiosks into ovens. Their colourful stall windows are propped open on sticks, revealing their wares. Sweets, cigarettes, chewing gum and assorted goods, all offered at 'unbeatable prices' promised by hand-written signs in Portuguese. The shop purveyors sit outside under the narrow shade of the building, drinking beer. It's poor, but far from miserable. Unlike Johannesburg, there appears to be no tension, no tangible hostility. I don't even lock the doors when the taxi stops at the first traffic light. Instead I roll down my window and relax.

My experience of Johannesburg is that life happens indoors: you travel from one gated community to another. Most restaurants and shops are housed in climate-controlled malls. You don't drive or sleep with your windows open. You don't walk anywhere. If you have money, you can spend a long time in Johannesburg without actually feeling the African sun or breathing the African air. The atmosphere of moneyed Johannesburg is regulated air-conditioning. Maputo, though, is sticky hot. Through the open car window I inhale the foreign smells and listen to the sing-song of Portuguese. For the first time in a long time, I feel like I'm in Africa.

When I arrive at my hostel I buy a local SIM card and call Willem straight away. He is driving to pick up his friend Ninette at the Swazi border and asks me if I'd like to come along. Ninette is also an Afrikaner, and went to journalism school with Willem in Pretoria. She now works as a reporter at one of the state papers in Swaziland and is visiting Willem for the weekend.

We're a little late and when we arrive we find the dark-haired Ninette waiting outside the border station. She is wearing a black dress with a bright-red belt and red high-heeled shoes. The nails of her fingers and toes are painted to match and she is wearing heavy make-up. Standing in the sun, high heels on the dusty gravel, she looks out of place and uncomfortable. She also looks high maintenance, like someone who would probably be irritated by tardiness. But if she is upset with us, she does not let on. Her appearance is nothing like what I imagined, perhaps because Willem described her as an idealist.

Ninette left South Africa pretty much immediately after graduating from journalism school because she wanted to 'work in Africa'. Like many Afrikaners she does not consider South Africa to be part of Africa. Her mission in *real* Africa is to write about important issues; to make a difference. However, working at one of Swaziland's two state-controlled papers, she has little say or influence and finds herself writing more about liposuction than social problems. She signed a two-year contract and has one year to go—a year she is not too excited about.

'People hardly speak English,' she exclaims indignantly as we stop for a cool drink at a café near the border.

Willem stays behind in the car to conduct a prescheduled phone interview, leaving Ninette and I to get to know one another.

'And they have sex all the time with different partners!' she adds.

Ninette recently discovered that a number of Swazi students were selling sex in order to buy food, and she rushed to her editors with the idea for a story. Her colleagues dismissed her, shrugging their shoulders and replying: 'We all do.' For the journalists it was not a matter of survival; they weren't standing on street corners. They traded sex for luxuries that their salaries couldn't cover, things like expensive clothing and hair extensions.

Ninette still struggles with the idea. Especially in a country that has the highest HIV prevalence rate in the world: 26 per cent.[1]

'Now, whenever someone comes to the office in a pretty new dress, I feel sick,' she says.

The attitude of the Swazis towards sex comes up a lot during our conversation. Like the archetypal 'good Afrikaner', Ninette does not believe in premarital sex, and in Swaziland she finds both dating and making friends extremely difficult when her underlying value system is so different. As a result she spends what little free time she has by herself.

A few weeks ago, Ninette was sexually assaulted by the security guard in her apartment building. She has been in therapy and is starting to feel a little better. However, she says it's tough to cast judgement because culturally, he really didn't do anything wrong. In a country with a king who literally grabs any virgin he wants at the annual Reed Dance, adding her to his harem of wives (at least thirteen thus far), there is little understanding for her position. She hopes a weekend with her friend in Maputo will cheer her up. At least she'll get some understanding and a sympathetic ear. The Afrikaner stance on sexuality is vastly different from that of the Swazi people. Willem has two sisters, yet it wasn't until university that he learnt what a tampon was. Those things are not something one talks about, he tells me. Nor is sex. While not all Afrikaner men abstain, their sexual experience is certainly very limited when they marry, he claims.

Willem is still a virgin. He says he looks at porn occasionally, but always feels guilty about it afterwards. In his opinion about half of all young Afrikaners today wait until marriage for their sexual debut.

'I believe in waiting, but a lot fewer people wait than say they do. Some of the boys at my school slept around,' he reveals.

The hypocrisy of Afrikaners upsets him, and Willem often feels betrayed by his culture and its rules.

'You have to believe what you believe because you considered it and accepted it, not just because you were taught to believe something,' he says.

Willem was born in 1987. He grew up unaware of apartheid or the pass laws.

'There was always a maid, always somebody cleaning,' he remembers. 'But they were just there. You knew they had a family somewhere and children somewhere, but somehow it was normal that they didn't see them. I was a little master of the maid. The maid could be cross with me but I could still tell her what to do.'

Willem's birth parents died when he was four. He was raised by his aunt and uncle, whom he refers to as his parents.

He has vague memories of the 1994 elections being big, but back then he didn't understand why. Anxiety was in the air. People were worried. Nobody knew what to expect. But it would take another couple of years before he realised what the furore was all about.

'The first time I realised that black people were regarded as a problem was in 1996 when our school got its first black boy. I still remember him: he had very thin legs and was the son of somebody's domestic worker,' Willem says.

The boy was in grade one and Willem was in grade three. Before the black student arrived at the school the principal summoned all the pupils for a talk. He told them there was a black boy coming and that it was 'normal'. But if it was normal, why had they all been summoned for a talk, Willem remembers wondering.

'As soon as he arrived, I realised he was different. You hadn't grasped you were living in an all-white society. Then this boy comes and all of a sudden you notice it.'

That was about as much reflection as he had time for before Willem was transferred to an all-boys school in Pretoria. It was an old, very traditional school and, like most other Afrikaans schools, it resented changing the way history was taught.

'It was supposed to be more nuanced, but the teachers made a joke of apartheid, always ridiculing and patronising. My history teacher taught more about how we suffered during the Anglo-Boer War than he did of apartheid. In fact, he never spoke of it. And now we're back at playing the victim for how we are being treated. We're good at that.'

By the time he was thirteen years old Willem was well schooled in racial prejudice.

'Blacks were said to be dangerous and so you distrusted them. The fear carried over. A lot of it was through stories of people being robbed or assaulted by blacks. My parents still can't tell a story without starting with *three black men* ...' says Willem. Then, as if feeling a little guilty about betraying them, he adds: 'My parents have changed a lot though.'

'Would you consider your parents racist?' I ask him.

'Racism is a really unhelpful term. It's too broad. Is a racist someone who hates black people or someone who thinks they are better than them? My parents are afraid of black people and think they are better than them. Whites are good. Blacks are evil. When they get crossed by a white person they'll say, "Can you believe that a white person did this to me?" But when my mom had surgery and had very nice black nurses she said, "They are not all bad. There are some nice ones."'

Willem says his parents believe black people are predisposed to evil acts and, as such, they expect to be treated badly by them—even robbed.

'There are certain things they still say that I hate—like Kaffir. Kaffir has become a really bad word. You can lose your job for saying it. Even at a party, off camera. But I imagine black South Africans have their collection of words for us too.'

But a lot of the prejudice is based on class as well, according to Willem.

'We have this expression for a lazy person; *kaffersleg*, meaning as bad as a Kaffir. It's what you call a white person who can't get ahead in life,' says Willem.

And people who belong to that category aren't exactly welcome in most Afrikaner households either.

'We'll donate a lot of money, but don't come visit,' says Willem.

He says in his parents' house, class would come before race: 'An educated, black, middle-class person, who came for dinner, would make my mom feel inferior. She'd be intimidated and nervous about speaking English,' he tells me.

Someone thought to be *kaffersleg*, however, would not be invited to dinner in the first place.

Willem's parents came from a poor background. His dad was an orphan, abandoned by his parents who were too poor to manage their thirteen kids. He never went to university, but as was expected of a good Afrikaner, he worked hard, eventually becoming an accountant. Now he is retired, but Willem's mother still has a teaching job. Willem says he grew up poor, but, like in all good Afrikaner families, the Calvinist work ethic permeated the home and ensured slow but steady progress.

'I'm critical of my parents, but also extremely proud of them for having come where they are today. They didn't come there on fat salaries, but by being very careful with their money. My mom was always doing something else, something extra to make extra money. Even though they benefitted from the system, their work ethic was very strong.'

I ask Willem about the importance of religion in his life; he is silent for a long time before he answers: 'There's religion and then there's faith.'

For Willem, faith is about belief, whereas religion is about culture. While, at the age of twenty-four, Willem is a modern Afrikaner, he still associates Afrikaner religious practices with the core cultural values of compliance, hard work, supporting the community, chastity and segregation—not mixing with black people because God has a different plan for them.

* * *

Back in Maputo, whole walls of colourful textiles draped over clotheslines flutter in the breeze as we pass by the craft market at Praça 25 de Junho. Paintings and artisan jewellery are spread out on the ground. Ninette finds the sellers 'too hectic' so we don't stay long; instead we head down to Avenida Marginal, and wander the waterfront in search of some of Mozambique's famous shrimp and a few beers. In Johannesburg I've missed being close to the sea. The salty breeze feels good in my nostrils and my lungs. I take deep breaths and stare out into the vastness that is the Indian Ocean. The afternoon sun enhances the colours and blurs the imperfections.

On the beach that runs parallel to Avenida Marginal, some locals are putting on an impromptu gospel performance. Their beautiful voices resonate in the air. I'm happy to note that no tourist sunbathers line the beach. Willem tells me most Westerners consider the water too dirty to swim here. They prefer to drive to the more remote and exclusive beach resorts. But the locals don't seem to care. Few know how to swim anyway and they seem content with staying by the water's edge. For them, the beach is not for tanning: it is a social arena; a place where life happens. Vendors come here to do business. Children come here to play. Adolescents come here to flirt. And evangelical churches, like the one this choir belongs to, come here to worship.

Willem and Ninette are hungry. Reluctantly I move on, accompanying them to a little restaurant on the beach. Once we are comfortably seated, I realise the local flavor has faded. Looking around I notice we are surrounded by white foreigners. To our left is a table of loud American aid workers; behind us is a group of fair-skinned French-speakers. I'm back in the safe and predictable bubble of ex-pats and expense accounts.

We move from one bubble to another as Willem invites me along to dinner at his friend Hanne's house. Hanne works at the Norwegian embassy. When we arrive at her gated apartment complex, two Canadians and an Australian aid worker have already arrived. Then Vincent, a Frenchman, shows up. We're now quite a multicultural crowd, but still there is not a single Mozambican. The air-conditioning even keeps the African heat at bay to the point where I feel like I might as well be in London or New York. Mozambique, like much of Africa, has become a place where the internationals advocating for the rights of the disadvantaged often live as segregated from them as possible.

Although he moved to Maputo to get to know the *real* Africa, Willem finds himself mainly spending time with the same clique of foreign correspondents, embassy employees, aid workers and international corporates, enjoying local culture without necessarily hanging out with locals.

'Being from different social backgrounds can be hard. I've grown resentful of the Scandinavian countries and their support systems. You'll meet 26-year-olds who don't know what they want to do with their lives and that is considered fine. I resent that they have that security,' he says.

For Willem, dawdling about in such a manner is out of the question. He once had to borrow money from his parents and felt his masculinity take a blow for it. As an Afrikaner you are expected to manage your life at all times, to make the hard decisions.

'*'n Boer maak 'n plan*, a Boer makes a plan—that encapsulates so much. You solve the problem,' says Willem. 'The thing I'm most afraid of in life is being poor. It seems to me undignified.'

Finding friends from Mozambique and breaking out of the racial silos is proving difficult, even though Willem speaks excellent Portuguese. He feels there is an underlying imbalance in economics and interests. He senses that locals always want something from him. And there's nothing to talk about. When spending time together, he says he simply can't relax.

'How should I associate with a black South African or Mozambican? What do we have in common? We don't like the same music or movies. I like discussing ideas. Maybe if I found that I could really talk to someone ...'

Willem has never dated a black woman, and although he has entertained the thought of doing so, he is pessimistic: 'I don't think it would work unless we came from the same civilisation.'

He feels it runs deeper than skin colour and boils down to a common cultural frame of reference. Although that is an excuse that was widely abused during apartheid, Willem still believes it to be true. To prove his point he says there is a black American woman at his work place that he would love to get to know better.

'It makes me wonder: why is it so much harder for me to associate with a Mozambican or a black South African?' he says.

But he settles on the explanation that black African culture is so radically different from his.

'I get along better with Asians than with Africans, maybe because I have less prejudice about Asians. I can see them more objectively because I didn't grow up around them and haven't been exposed to as much prejudice. When it comes to Africans, I come with all my historical baggage. I'm well-meaning. I want to embrace somebody for who they are, despite their background, but I know that I come from this white, frontier farmer background. That has influenced me and I hate that. Somehow I have assimilated the prejudices. Some I believe to be true, some I know aren't true, but I still believe them,' he says.

'So what are the prejudices you believe to be true?' I ask.

'I do believe that Africans have a more relaxed working culture. I believe that they now have a sense of entitlement. And I do believe certain laws are used to punish whites.'

'And what do you know isn't true but still believe?'

'That they are out to get me. There is this frontier mentality. We're waiting for the barbarians. You seek things out that confirm your fears.'

I ask Willem about his take on violent crime against white people in South Africa.

'It's problematic because being white usually means you have more money. But it's not as simple as that. If you want attention in South Africa, you are violent. We have a culture of violence. Presenting a memorandum doesn't work, so you become violent: you burn stuff, hurt and humiliate. Raping a seventy-year-old can't be because you're attracted to her,' he says.

Willem thinks it's only natural that frustration and resentment build when, for so many people, nothing has changed.

'How can someone not be resentful after so many years of mistreatment? I just have to think of the resentment I feel for

Scandinavians, fat cats, or nepotism among high-ranking black officials. It makes me boil with anger when somebody is appointed because of their allegiances, not competencies. I realise that this must have been the reality during apartheid as well. If I'm resentful about these things how much more so would I feel if I were a black farm worker and nothing had changed for me? That's why if I go to a farm I expect the workers to be hostile. I feel ashamed to speak Afrikaans even when they can't speak English. I'm a representative of this culture they must hate. I report on the ANC Youth League and I feel intimidated. Do I expect them to kill me? No. But I expect them to resent me. Great injustice was done to them, they must be angry.'

I ask Willem if he feels guilty about apartheid even though he didn't live through it. There is no hesitation in his forceful nod of agreement.

'We don't want to talk about it. Somebody who says apartheid is in the past is someone who hasn't confronted apartheid. It still dictates the route your life will take. It's part of who we are and the way we do things. For many whites nothing has changed since apartheid except sometimes they don't have water and there are potholes.'

Willem believes that he, like every other Afrikaner, carries the collective guilt of apartheid, even though he was born as it was coming to an end.

'I still benefitted from the system. I started school in 1994, but the system didn't just change like that. I benefitted from privileges that the system protected. Even my children will carry the guilt because they too will go to a school that has an institutional memory.'

He fears that if he can't find a way to get over the guilt he will pass it on to them.

Willem believes that white South Africans will become less and less prominent in general. At least he hopes so. Perhaps it would ease the guilt.

16 DECEMBER 2011

A TALE OF TWO MUSEUMS

'Isn't it great that you can be here and experience Afrikaner culture with us,' Revd Pieter Bester says to me.

He makes a broad gesture with his arms indicating the delicious food, the burning braai spreading its light and heat, and the circle of folk musicians playing traditional Afrikaans songs on accordion and guitar.

While the word braai translates to barbeque, it is so much more than that. In South Africa, a braai is a cultural ritual dating back to the days when trekkers roamed the interior, catching their own game with a single bullet or with a bow and arrow when ammunition ran low. Then they'd roast the meat right there, on the open field, under the African sky.

All day long the Hugo brothers have served me meat. Carlo has just offered me a rum and Coke. I feel like I am in the hands of the best of hosts.

'But you know it's only 'cause you're white ... If you had been a black reporter, this wouldn't have been possible,' Revd Bester continues. 'You're not Afrikaner. Really, you are as much of an outsider as they are, you just don't look like one. It's a shame, really, that it has to be like that.'

Pieter Bester is the young pastor of a congregation in the town of Standerton in Mpumalanga, about two hours from the battle site of Blood River. He describes the community as somewhat right-wing, but despite his initial expectations, he is quite happy there. Bester is attending the Blood River celebrations for the first time. He came hoping to influence the event—to encourage the people attending it to be more open-minded. He brought along his four-year-old son.

'I have never taught him the difference between white and black,' he tells me. 'But today he came back to the tent after playing, and said: "We have to kill the Zulus because they are our enemies." It made me very sad. He doesn't know what a Zulu is, but still.'

Blood River is a symbol of resistance to both Zulu and Afrikaner alike. For Afrikaners, the Voortrekkers showed unrivalled bravery and piousness here, laying the foundation for the creation of a *volk* with its own unique history and ideology. For Zulu people, the battle is regarded as their first major opposition to white invasion and colonial aggression.

On the other side of the river, a community centre is being built next to the Ncome Museum. Cecilia Kruger, of the Heritage Foundation in Pretoria, calls it 'a huge modern construction, defacing the battlefield.'

'You can't even see the circle of wagons anymore. They are completely obliterated by the new buildings behind. I don't know how they got it past the environmental-impact people,' she says.

According to Kruger, by 2012, the government had spent some 40 million rand on construction of the Ncome Museum and an additional 20 million rand would be needed to complete construction.

'Meanwhile, the Blood River side gets no funding,' she says. 'If one had reconciled properly, one would have used existing institutions and built on that instead.'

'You should go over. See for yourself,' Jacques Hugo tells me.

He is soundly unimpressed with the new Ncome museum and the 16 December Reconciliation Day celebrations currently taking place there. He says the drumming is often so loud that it disrupts the religious services of the Afrikaners. And to make matters worse, the government pays for the party, donating truckloads of beer and whole cattle to the commemorations, and thus effectively sponsoring an all-night party. Meanwhile, on the other side of the river, the Afrikaners receive nothing, not even a grant for their museum, which is run entirely on private donations.

'Have you been?' I ask him.

He hasn't. Nor does he have an interest in going. Relations have deteriorated too much, he claims: 'We respected each other but the respect was taken away. The blacks have been told we stole their land. This land was bought from the Zulu king and the Zulu farmers came here to look for jobs. It was *bought*, never taken, but nowadays children are told that us whites came here to steal the land.'

Jacques is disappointed that the Zulu people have changed the stories that are passed on to younger generations.

'People are brought up under the wrong impression,' he exclaims indignantly. 'The older Zulus know the land has been bought. It's their fault the younger ones hate us, because they stopped teaching them what really happened and now all they hear is how the whites stole from them.'

Looking across the plains you can clearly see a colourful dance festival underway. The two museums are situated a mere stone's throw from each other, but to get from one to the other requires a 3 km detour on dirt roads, to a small service bridge further down the river.

About a thousand people have gathered to watch performances of traditional Zulu and Sotho dance. Most are dressed in traditional outfits, adorned with elaborate beadwork. Younger girls are bare-chested, while older married women wear *isidwaba*, a traditional leather skirt. My arrival causes a few surprised looks from the crowd—but there is no hostility. Several people approach to welcome me. Some even clap. It doesn't take me long to realise that this is not the wild party Jacques described. The dancing is part of a cultural competition, a daytime event running until 4 pm. Though there is a free lunch buffet for visitors, I don't see any cases of free beer. In a big tent dance performances are under way. A few other white people are scattered in the crowd: a representative of the Voortrekker/Msunduzi Museum in Pietermaritzburg; Cecilia Kruger; another journalist; and someone else I don't recognise.

I try to talk to some people outside. Younger people seem suspicious of my presence and won't answer my greetings, but the older ones are more welcoming. As I wander the grounds, almost every question I'm asked relates to the other side of the river: What goes on there? Have you been? Is there a huge party? Is it bigger than ours? Why can't we hear their music? Why aren't we welcome?

When I enter the museum, a young black journalist lights up at the sight of me. She and an accompanying photographer rush over hoping for an interview. She, too, wants to know if I've been to 'the other side'. What is it like? What do people do 'over there'? Wouldn't it be so much nicer if everyone could celebrate together?

'Why aren't blacks welcome?' she asks.

'There is no rule against black people visiting,' I tell her, but then I remember the stories I've heard, and quickly add: 'But contact the management first, just so you have someone to accompany you ... in case.'

The few black people who have ventured to the other side have not always had pleasant experiences. On 16 December 2008, some people working at the Ncome site decided to start their commemorations on the other side. They had intended to stay for an hour and a half, but allegedly felt so threatened that they left after just 35 minutes.

'I am not bitter, but I *am* disappointed,' the program director, Mzi Mngadi, said in a speech on the Ncome side later that same day.[1]

And last year a black photographer was reportedly told 'Fuck off, Kaffir!' when he attempted to photograph one of the religious ceremonies on the Blood River Site.

This year, the only black person I saw at the Blood River Site was Sam Nzima, the photojournalist known for his iconic picture of Hector Pieterson, taken at the 1976 Soweto uprising. While Nzima told me he was having a pleasant visit, he kept his distance and stayed accompanied by management.

Revd Bester thinks it's a shame that so many people make Blood River a political thing.

'Why does it have to be a "we won"? We made a pact with God to not let us die. It's between us and God and has nothing to do with the Zulus. There were even black people helping us,' he says.

27

AFRICA'S WHITE TRIBE

'We're Africans since the seventeenth century. Not everyone accepts that. They still see us as colonial intruders—Europeans who are not really indigenous to Africa, even though our roots here stretch three to four hundred years back.

'I'm fifth or sixth generation African. This is my homeland and my forefathers have been in South Africa just as long as many of the black tribes have been here. Only the Khoikhoi and the San people were here before.

'We are the white tribe of Africa and I want my people to understand that we have just as much right to be here. Once Africa gets under your skin, nothing can replace it.'

The voice of Reverend Schalk Albertyn is much too powerful for the modest room that has become his office. I meet him in a place where neither he nor any of his friends or family members imagined an anti-apartheid activist would ever set foot—Orania. Yet the reverend exudes earnestness; his new quest is so unlikely that it must be genuine.

Revd Albertyn had spent eight years working at different supermarkets when he was finally offered a position with a congregation in Kimberley. There he remained on a temporary contract until one day, in 2011, he received a phone call asking if he would come preach an Easter service in Orania. At first he wasn't sure.

'I thought Orania was made up of a group of people who wanted the old apartheid system back; that it would be an Amish-like community. So when I was invited here to preach I thought long and hard about it. I didn't even know what to preach to these people,' he tells me.

Finally, he accepted. That weekend he had many long and intense discussions with the community leadership. To his surprise, he found that Orania was nothing like what he had expected. He was so enthralled that he decided to relocate.

Knowing the community couldn't afford a full-time minister, Revd Albertyn offered to become a tentmaking minister; that is, to take other employment in order to make a living. He applied for a position as head of community services, responsible for a wide range of areas ranging from welfare and health services to discipline, mediation and arbitration.

He got the job and, in July 2011, he and his family moved to Orania.

'This is a strange place, not a normal society. It's a society built on a political idea; a people who want to sustain themselves and work towards achieving something excellent. What bothered me the most about apartheid was the notion that we are better than others and so they should do our labour. Here, we are working ourselves to achieve our ideals, not on the back of someone else,' he says.

Albertyn's friends were shocked when he told them he was moving to Orania.

'"*You*, in *Orania*?" they said with disbelief. They saw me as someone who wouldn't fit in. I had been involved in so many cultural groups advocating the rights of others that many thought I was actually against my own people. It was a surprise for them to find that I could also identify with my own people,' he tells me.

Revd Albertyn believes that South Africa's current political leadership is alienating people from each other and practising a kind of 'apartheid in reverse'.

'Apartheid goes against the gospel. I very much supported the end of apartheid. I wanted equality—for South Africa to be a place for all. But it didn't happen that way. The new leaders just empowered their own people,' he says.

'I have always seen myself as a champion of the underdog. And the people who are being discriminated against now are the white people, especially the Afrikaners. The government is trying to annihilate our history and replace it. Doing exactly what the Afrikaners were criticised for doing before, when nothing was taught about black history. I sympathise with the idea of having a peaceful place for Afrikaners to live out their culture. It is not safe out there and it's not easy for ordinary white people to get jobs. There is widespread racism against white people. These people need somebody to support them and help them.'

An important reason for choosing to move to Orania was the reverend's desire to lead Orania in a positive direction.

'Being a reverend is a powerful position, one can influence a lot,' he says.

But he also realises that things will take time and he regards his work here as a long-term commitment.

'The work is very challenging,' he tells me. 'It's a new community—one that is being built from scratch—but the congregation has accepted me very well. People who come here do so sacrificing a lot of things in order to build something new. There's a pioneer spirit here. Everybody is still in survival mode.'

Albertyn believes that his most important task is to help people accept themselves, to accept the fact that they are part of Africa. To not live in the past and be negative about what is happening to the Afrikaner in South Africa, but to find a new future with a new ideal and to work towards that ideal.

'Many feel that they are not given an opportunity to stay and better themselves in Africa. In Orania they can say, "This is our own place. We belong here and we have a role to play." South Africa will always be culturally diverse and we need people to accept that and to accept each other,' he says.

But the reverend does not believe that segregation is a long-term solution: 'I see Orania as an intermeasure for the Afrikaner people to find themselves again and to find new hope. I don't believe it should be permanent, but for the moment it is a viable option to stabilise the culture and the future, because the Afrikaner is so very vulnerable at the moment.'

But while Albertyn regards Orania as a temporary safe haven for Afrikaners, the rest of management clearly envisions something much more permanent. The reverend informs me that 4,000 hectares of additional land has already been purchased on the West Coast. The idea is that the concept of Orania will be implemented there, and that the two areas will eventually be physically connected via an overland corridor, providing the whole territory with sea access.

Carel Boshoff does not want to confirm any such plans, but speaks of this newly acquired land as a 'holiday community' obtained by individuals with ties to the Orania Company. Perhaps he fears that too bold a growth strategy will place Orania in the limelight, and spark resistance from the South African government.

There are fourteen Christian churches in Orania, each of different denomination and with varying degrees of orthodoxy. With its eighty to ninety members, Revd Albertyn's Dutch Reformed Church services just over 10 per cent of the community. The largest church, with about a hundred and twenty members, is the Afrikaans Protestant Church, an ultra-right-wing church that split away from the Dutch Reformed Church when the latter announced it no longer supported apartheid. There are also a number of small, very conservative, Christian churches.

'The British-Israelites believe that people of European heritage—which includes Afrikaners—are direct descendants of the Lost Tribes of ancient Israel. They don't regard black people as human beings, but consider them to be on the same level as animals. Nor do they accept large parts of the New Testament, but live and worship according to the Old Testament. They hold some extremely racist ideas,' say Albertyn.

The reverend believes the existence of racism is especially widespread among people who came to Orania because they had witnessed or been victims of violent crime.

He realises that conquering the hearts and minds of all Oranians will be difficult, but he is up for the challenge.

'You don't change people by acquiring members for your church. You change people by getting them to accept their humanity. The first thing people lose when they become oppressed is their self-respect and their value as human beings. In the apartheid days it was the blacks who needed to regain this. If you can't respect yourself you can't respect others. By preaching that God accepts them as they are and that he forgives them the wrongs they have done, I try to make people see that they too have value, a place under the sun, a role to play. If they feel that God forgives them and regards them as worthy then they'll start respecting themselves as well.'

28

ORANIA REVISITED

In April 2012, I return to C-block unannounced, expecting to see the same ramshackle rows of buildings that I saw when I was last here six months ago. But C-block looks nothing like it used to. New, decent-sized rooms have replaced the 'stables'. It's still basic, but the rebuilt walls have some insulation—and it's clean. Everything has been reconstructed and at remarkable speed, considering no outside labour is used.

About seven years ago, when the concept of singles' quarters was first introduced in Orania, the turnover was massive. Some five hundred men would come and go in a year. Then, after introducing the policy of no alcohol or drugs, the situation improved—but still many drifters cycle through. Over the course of 2011, eighty newcomers arrived and left.

'They wake up one day and decide they can't take it anymore,' says Dawid, the C-block shopkeeper. 'Some arrive with nothing but the clothes on their backs, not even a plastic bag or an ID. We give them a bed and a few things.'

I find Dawid in new facilities, around the corner from where he used to be. The size of his little store has multiplied and he is in the process of building a restaurant. He is thrilled to see me and immediately offers to cook me dinner, for which he refuses to charge.

'Is Fransie still around?' I ask.

'No, he left last year. Went nuts, packed his bags—or I guess he only had the one bag—and left. He was always a little nuts. Used to walk around telling people he was a colonel, but of course he never was.'

'Who was he then?'

'Ag, who knows ... Some guy who'd been living on the streets for too long. We get a lot of those guys here. They make up all sorts of stories. Some even start to believe them themselves.'

'But his stories were so convincing, down to the smallest detail.'

'Not everything he said was true, that's for sure. There were conversations with guys who were on the border in the same places Fransie claims to have been, and he didn't know the names of people or places he should have known if he had actually been there,' says Dawid.

If Fransie was a con artist he was a brilliant one. I decide to call up John Strydom at the Orania Movement, a member of the team that interviews and does background checks on all prospective residents. I figure he must know the truth about Fransie.

'Fransie may very well have been a colonel, we have no way of knowing. He's one of those guys who comes and goes,' Strydom tells me.

Apparently there are no records of Fransie anywhere.

I hang up and return to my visit with Dawid. He is dishing out food to workers who have arrived famished after a long day of manual labour. His store is as crowded as ever. Last time I saw Dawid, he told me he wouldn't extend credit. But as we're standing, chatting away in his store, I see it happen more than once. He won't give away tobacco or sweets, but no one is refused a meal, whether they can pay for it or not.

'Guy's hungry ... they work hard all day long out there,' he says—and looks away, almost embarrassed. 'I still do alright. I make enough of a profit,' he adds.

After a while, the silence that characterises Orania is broken by the sound of an engine. It's an approaching motorbike, accelerating as it travels along the straight stretch of road leading up to Dawid's shop. As it approaches, it slows down and finally comes to a halt outside. The driver enters the shop and takes off his helmet. It's Riaan, the quiet guy with the protruding ears who showed me his C-block unit the last time I visited. Back then he used to ride an old blue bicycle, but he seems to have upgraded to this shining red monster.

'You here again?' he says, and his face breaks open into a big smile.

Then he quickly covers his mouth, as if just remembering that he has no front teeth. Like a teenager with braces, he tries his best to get through the rest of the conversation smiling only with his mouth closed.

'I have a proper flat now,' he tells me, visibly proud. 'Do you want to see it?'

'I'd love to!' I reply.

He rushes out and disappears into the night.

'Where did he go?' I ask Dawid.

'To make his bed, no doubt,' Dawid laughs.

* * *

I step outside and walk along the edge of the building until I see light streaming out from an open door. I peak inside. Riaan is sitting on his bed. With the concentration and effort of a first grade student, he is busy writing something on a piece of paper.

The room is certainly bigger than the last one: at least three times the size. While he still doesn't have his own toilet or shower, he does have a few chairs and a small table with Orania's flag for tablecloth. The bed is the same iron bed he used to have, but now covered with more blankets and with a new bedside table at its side. On the wall above his bed hangs a picture of a pony. It looks like one of those posters that sometimes accompany childrens' magazines; it even has PONY written in big pink letters at the top.

Riaan sees me standing in the doorway and lights up. He stands up, motions for me to come inside, and hands me the piece of paper. On it, his name and email address are neatly printed in big childish letters.

'Maybe you could write to me sometime,' he says.

He stretches out his arm and points to the corner of the room, where the big trophy sits: a brand new computer placed carefully on a small desk.

'I have Internet now,' he beams. 'Maybe we could be friends on Facebook?'

He has given up trying to cover his mouth. He is just too happy. There is too much to be excited about.

'How do you write your name?' he asks me. But continues before I get a chance to tell him: 'Wait. Don't tell me. I'll find you.'

His ears turn red as he adds: 'There can only be one face like yours out there.'

I walk back to Dawid's store, stopping to blink away a few unexpected tears before entering. The store is quiet now.

'Wow, Riaan has really moved up in the world,' I say to Dawid.

'Ja, he works hard,' Dawid says. 'Do you know his story? ... He has a drinking problem. His daughter died in a car accident because he was driving drunk and after that his bottom fell out. Now he's trying to get to a place where he will at least be allowed to see his son again.'

Broken-hearted, drunk and broke, Riaan roamed South Africa in desperate need of work. Waiting to hitch his next ride, he finally collapsed not far from the turn-off to Orania. Someone found him lying there on the pavement and brought him in. That was about a year ago; he hasn't left since.

As I'm sitting there chatting with Dawid, it turns out there are many more backstories that I didn't know.

'Do you remember the big guy with red hair?' Dawid asks me. 'You know ... the guy who rides around on his bike saying *broom-broom* and pretending it's a motorcycle. You met him last time you were here ...'

I search my brain, trying to recall. The big guy with red hair? I remember now ... He was part of the group of guys who cornered me in Dawid's store one night, asking whether Swedish women found black men attractive and, if so, how that was possible. I remember feeling uncomfortable. They were standing too close and kept reaching out to touch my hair. Their comments were racist, their jokes crude, and I remember having to work hard to hide my feelings of disgust. The big guy with red hair didn't say much, and I never spoke to him directly, but I remember feeling scared of him. He was massive in size and there was an air of unpredictability about him.

'Yes, I know who you mean,' I tell Dawid.

'He is 22, but has the mental capacity of a 10-year-old. Sad story, really ... His mom died when he was a baby, so he was raised by his abusive and alcoholic dad who eventually drank himself to death. Only no one knew. Then one day a black lady hears children crying and enters the farmhouse. She finds the boy and his brother with the decomposing corpse of their father. So she takes them home to raise them, but leaves the corpse be—doesn't call the police or nothing. Then one day a white lady driving past notices the white kids among the black family and stops to check things out. She finds the rotten body and calls the police. The kids are taken away and raised in different foster homes.

'The brother, who is nineteen, has the mental capacity of a six-year-old. They never stood a chance. Now in Orania they have work and a place to sleep, but there are no resources to provide the psychiatric care they obviously need. The big guy can get quite violent. He's a kid. All he wants is a hug at night and for someone to say they love him. Instead you get a lot of the guys picking on him. It's sad really,' says Dawid.

Psychiatric help is something many of the residents at the singles' quarters could benefit from. But it's just not available. In Orania discipline is the tool used to help people better themselves. If the discipline slacks, you're out. Everyone gets a chance no matter their past, but only one. However, according to Dawid, this is slowly starting to change. Much of this is thanks to Revd Albertyn, who sits on the disciplinary committee and who tends to argue in favour of second chances.

'The new reverend is very softhearted,' says Dawid. 'He doesn't believe in treating people like dirt. He is all for trying to change a guy rather than kicking him out. And if you can't change someone, then accept him the way he is as long as he is not a threat to society.'

There is a security team to help break up fights if arguments become violent. If it gets totally out of hand the police from Hopetown are called in, but only as a last resort. Nobody in Orania likes seeing black policemen 'whacking whites'.

Avoiding calling in the police is one of the main reasons for the no-drinking policy. At first I thought it silly that the men had to be controlled to the point where they couldn't even have a beer, but when I hear how widespread alcoholism and drug abuse is, I understand the logic. Many of these men can't have 'just one beer' and with no resources for therapy, not even support groups like Alcoholics Anonymous, complete abstinence, discipline and hard work is likely the only chance they have of pulling through. Many leave, they just can't do it anymore: working is hard, stealing is easier.

In the past month, three guys have been kicked out and two of the new arrivals have left of their own volition. Corné is gone, too. He was caught breaking into a car to steal money.

'He went back to his old ways,' Dawid says.

* * *

Terrence is still around though. He arrives straight from the rugby field one evening to buy pizza. He is sweaty with grass and dirt on his legs, but wearing shiny white rugby shorts, so new that he forgot to cut off the price tag. He seems taller. His eyes are clear and white, not red and foggy like they were six months ago. He still doesn't say much, just gives me a quick nod and a smile, but it makes me happy to see that he is still here and thriving. There are some new faces, too—like Charl, whose sister married a real estate agent and moved to America.

'She has even been to Paris. I'm so jealous,' he says, but with a proud smile.

'You should go see her,' I reply.

'Yeah, she keeps telling me to come, but I'm too scared,' he smiles.

He tells me he is twenty-eight, but he looks younger. He works hard all day long. And at night he works extra in Dawid's shop as an electrician. He's trying to acquire the skills to set up a business of his own. Maybe then he can go to Paris one day, too. Or America.

* * *

As I'm leaving, I walk past Riaan's room to say goodbye. I take a seat in one of his chairs and absent-mindedly start fingering the old, worn Orania flag he uses for tablecloth.

Riaan watches me in silence for a few moments, then says: 'You can have it.'

Before I have time to object, he takes it off the table and carefully folds it. Then, using both hands in an act of great reverence, he hands it to me.

'Orania has been good to me,' he says.

29

A QUESTION OF SURVIVAL

The past is really almost as much a work of the imagination as the future.

Jessamyn West

When I have asked Afrikaner leaders about the key to understanding their people, the answer has always been the same: survival.

'Apartheid was wrong and cannot be justified in any way, but it was the Afrikaners' answer to the question of how do we survive: not how do we dominate or suppress, but how do we *survive*. It became corrupt, but the idea was not. We have fear and survival in our genes,' claims Tim du Plessis.

Survival has meant different things for the Afrikaners in different centuries. In the early years, survival meant physically surviving the hardships of a frontier life. With the arrival of the British it shifted to economic and political survival. In the apartheid era the term was abused, referring mainly to the protection of privilege. In recent years, the survivalist focus has shifted to culture and minority rights.

'At the core there is a notion that this culture and people must survive. But in a country like this, can you survive as the minority? How will we, and what we have built up, survive in the future? There are 6 per cent Afrikaners in South Africa. We built our entire identity around a language and a sense of history,' says Hermann Giliomee, Extraordinary Professor of History at the University of Stellenbosch.

And now that history is being rewritten and the language pushed out, the preservation of Afrikaans as a language is a major concern for survivalists. Although the language appears vibrant and there are plenty of arts and culture festivals, Giliomee makes a distinction between such consumption and what he refers to as *reproduction*, which deals with linguistic development and level of sophistication.

'Reproduction has to happen in education. There is only one truly Afrikaans-speaking university remaining of the twenty-two institutes for higher learning that there used to be. Even at Stellenbosch University we are fighting a battle. All postgraduate courses are in English. Once you abandon the language in the university it will have enormous effects on culture and literature,' he says.

It will take a long time before the Afrikaner becomes absorbed into black South Africa—if it ever happens at all. The cultural divide between them is too great. However, it is highly possible that, within a few generations, Afrikaners could be absorbed into English-speaking white culture. Many have already immigrated to different English-speaking countries like Great Britain, Australia, New Zealand and Canada. Even within South Africa, the trend is towards Anglo–Afrikaans integration. Giliomee's daughters have both married Englishmen. His grandchildren speak English at home. And while he has nothing against his sons-in-law, it's just one more example of cultural dilution. How many more generations will it take until the Afrikaners cease to be Afrikaners?

I remember the words of Carel Boshoff, President of the Orania Movement: 'A people is one generation deep. If one generation rejects itself you are lost.'

A QUESTION OF SURVIVAL

A survey conducted at Stellenbosch University in 2007 showed that nearly half of the Afrikaans-speaking students refrained from pressing their language rights because of the apartheid legacy.[1] Antjie Krog distilled this sentiment effectively in her 1998 book about the Truth and Reconciliation Commission, *Country of My Skull*: 'How do I live with the fact that all the words used to humiliate, all the orders given to kill, belonged to the language of my heart?'[2]

Some have even stopped teaching their children Afrikaans, preferring to speak English at home. A CEO of one of Africa's largest and most progressive firms told me he considered teaching his native language to his children 'a waste of grey matter,' as Afrikaans was such a small and dying language.

The language movement was an important part of forging Afrikaner unity and nationalism.[3] But there is little doubt that with a shrinking population, declining scholastic options, global irrelevancy in commerce, the stigma of apartheid and a growing use of English as a primary means of communication among South Africans, Afrikaans is a language with a troubled future.

'So what is the verdict, then? Do you think the Afrikaners will survive as a people?' I ask Giliomee.

'Will the Swedish survive?'

His question throws me off.

'Yes, of course they will ...' I respond somewhat hesitantly.

'For how long? A century? Two?'

Any country with an aging population that is only maintaining its growth thanks to immigration will sooner or later face the same challenges faced by Afrikaners. What steps are we prepared to take in order to survive as a people? How far are we prepared to go?

Most Afrikaners agree that it can no longer be about survival at any cost.

Already in the mid-1940s, an Afrikaans poet by the name of N.P. van Wyk Louw posed the question: 'Can a small *volk* survive for long, if it becomes something hateful, something evil, in the eyes of the best, in—or outside—its fold?' The *volk*, he said, ran the risk of losing the support of a critical number of its own intellectuals if it gave up on its quest for 'survival in justice' and settled for 'mere survival'.[4]

The philosophies and atrocities of apartheid have caused many, both around the world and across South Africa, to question whether Afrikaners even deserve to survive as a people. Today, the ghost of this doubt, reflected within the Afrikaner community itself, is perhaps the greatest threat to their survival.

* * *

When Tim du Plessis interviewed Nelson Mandela in 1992, Mandela tried to explain the difference between the Afrikaner and the British—as he saw it. He did so by telling Du Plessis a story that he had been told by his elders.[5] He said that if a hungry black man knocked on the door of a British home in search of food, the British Madam would open the door and ask him what she could do for him. And the black man would say: 'Sorry Madam, but I am very hungry. Do you have anything to eat?'

The British lady would invite him in and tell him to wait by the front door. She would then return with a cup of tea and a slice of bread with a little bit of butter on it. The tea would be weak and the slice of bread would be 'so thin you could see the sun shine through it,' but the black man would be allowed to stay by the front door to eat it.

However, if the black man knocked on the door of an Afrikaner home the Madam would open and say: 'What are you doing knocking on my front door? Go around to the back!' The man would go around to the back and knock again. The Madam would open and exclaim: 'What's your problem?!'

'I'm sorry Madam, but I am very hungry. Do you have anything to eat?' he would ask.

'Well, don't come into my house. Go sit down under that tree over there,' the Madam would reply, pointing to the backyard. Then, ten minutes later, she would return with a big jug of coffee with six teaspoons of sugar and five thick slices of bread with peanut butter and jam. She would also hand over a plastic bag with leftover food for the man to take home to his family.

After my time in South Africa, I still find Mandela's story a useful analogy for the spirit of the Afrikaner. Whether it's mending your tent or feeding you, it is very unlikely that an Afrikaner will leave you stranded. Afrikaners frequently treat individual black people with kindness and compassion, but can be cruel and callous when acting collectively to protect their own.

Du Plessis once told me that to understand is not to condone. Behind the word 'Afrikaner' stands a people who have lived through decades of social engineering; who have been brainwashed into internalising a value system manufactured by an elite with a very specific agenda. At school they were frequently taught exaggerations, fabrications, even outright lies. At home they were instructed on how to be good whites, down to the details of how they should fold their towels and organise their homes. They were subjected to constant supervision by their neighbours, family members, and the police state itself. They were raised on fear, and manipulated by it at the hands of their own leadership.

Yet, in spite of the fact that they represented less than ten per cent of the population, that the other ninety per cent had every reason to destroy them, many stood up to reject the past. Under the lead of President F.W. de Klerk, they laid down their arms and walked into an uncertain future.

Not everyone was able to follow Mandela's example and let bygones be bygones. There is still a great deal of bitterness among those black people for whom nothing has changed, and among those white people for whom the future looks increasingly dire. At the very moment when black South Africans should have leapt up to slit the throats of white South Africans, the revolution was suspended; the battle called off. Although praised internationally, this non-violent transition left many without a sense of closure. Black Africans were pressured by their morally superior leaders to walk away when they knew in their hearts they could have won, in fact, *should* have won. And the Afrikaners, who 'never go down without a fight,' were pressured to do just that: to lay down their arms, admit their wrongdoings and ask forgiveness for something they knew in their hearts was unforgivable.

'Once you lose credibility you can never get it back. It is such a dominant idea that people need to be recognised equally. Separate-but-equal is not equal. Those were the death words around anything to do with apartheid. And they were right; it was not equal,' concedes Carel Boshoff.

'After apartheid many people argued that we must kill the term Afrikaner, that it had been contaminated and would always be associated with apartheid,' states Tim du Plessis. 'We must get ourselves a new name, they said. We must change the brand. But you can call yourself whatever you want. People from the outside will look at you, listen to your accent, and they will immediately know you are an Afrikaner.'

Instead of finding a new name, Du Plessis feels it is time to give new content to the term. He'd like the Afrikaner people to become an admired progressive minority instead of being known as the 'people of apartheid'.

While that goal still appears to be a long way off, part of the Afrikaner intellectual elite are trying, this time openly, to save Afrikanerdom by renovating Afrikaner cultural identity, building on Afrikaner values suited for the realities of the new South Africa. At the core of this revitalised identity is self-reliance—*'n Boer maak 'n plan*. The little boy on the Orania flag, rolling up his sleeves ready to get to work, is perhaps the best symbol of this self-reliance. It seems relevant not only for the people of Orania, but for Afrikaners across the continent. It's an appeal to all Afrikaners to get over their revulsion for manual labour or *kafferwerk*. There will never be true equality and mutual respect if domestic workers and gardeners only exist in shades of black.

Just like affirmative action ensures younger generations of black people have role models with white-collar careers, white youths need to get used to seeing white petrol attendants, rubbish collectors and street sweepers. Many poor and uneducated Afrikaners I spoke to claimed they would prefer to starve rather than become the maid or gardener of a black middle-class family. If the Afrikaner is to survive, this attitude must change. Starting out by serving white families, like the manual labourers of Orania, might make the transition to these kinds of jobs a little bit easier for the average Afrikaner.

While Orania is frequently and rightfully criticised for entrenching the segregationist tendencies of the past, the case can also be made that in promoting complete self-reliance, fostering their culture, and encouraging Afrikaners to regain their dignity through hard labour, Orania serves as a potential stepping-stone to the realities of a new South Africa.

EPILOGUE

16 December 2011: Banks of Blood River

The storm never comes. The fortified camp the Hugo brothers built for me is never put to the test. And while the army of black clouds remains a menace, it is a distant one.

At dawn, Afrikaner families slowly wander down from the campground towards Blood River. Fair-skinned, fair-haired, some are dressed in traditional Voortrekker clothing.

Surrounded by a circle of sixty-four bronze wagons, a pastor holds a sermon. He reminds those who have gathered of the vow they have taken—the vow to commemorate 16 December as a holy day. He speaks about what happened here at Blood River; about how, at this very spot, God singled out the Afrikaners and let it be known that they are a chosen people. Old flags from the pre-union republics and the apartheid era are brought in on horses, and raised.

After the service I make my way down to the river's edge, walking along its banks until I come across three concrete pillars in the middle of the river. In 1998, the ANC government began the construction of a pedestrian bridge to connect the Afrikaner museum of Blood River to the Zulu museum of Ncome, with the aim of creating a united heritage site in the spirit of reconciliation. Three concrete piles were erected. Then construction stopped. But not for lack of funding, permits, or governmental will. I never get a straight answer as to why progress has ceased, but rumour has it there have been anonymous threats of explosions, flooding and sabotage. One thing is certain; the bridge is not welcome.

There is a difference between reconciliation and redefinition, between reaching out and reaching for, between embracing and engulfing. The Afrikaners, having watched their streets renamed, their history rewritten, their dates repurposed, their monuments reconciled, their race reclassified and their language retrenched, understand that the first guest across any bridge is assimilation. And so, they have retreated to their circle of wagons, their laager at Blood River.

Fourteen years later, the three pillars still stand, stubbornly resisting the current, as Blood River and time erode them to sand.

AFTERWORD

'We have gathered here today to celebrate the National Day of Reconciliation during an important year when we mark the twentieth anniversary of democracy and freedom,' President Jacob Zuma announces.[1]

It is 16 December 2014. The Reconciliation Bridge between Ncome and Blood River museums has finally been completed and Zuma is on site, hosting the inauguration.

'It is befitting that today we are gathering at a venue that has been the source of pain and conflict, and which caused the sixteenth of December to be commemorated in different ways in our country for many decades,' he continues. 'For some it was the symbol of triumph, for others, the symbol of resistance and pain or alternatively a bitter potent experience of wars and dispossession.'[2]

About two thousand people have arrived at Ncome Museum to celebrate the unveiling of the cylinder-like construction connecting the two sides of the river.[3] Its peculiar silver rings extend like a futuristic time machine built to teleport people from one side to the other.

A small contingent of Afrikaner cultural representatives made up of Voortrekker Museum manager, Etta Judson, Managing Director of the Voortrekker Monument, General Gert Opperman, and Cecilia Kruger of the Heritage Foundation, approach the bridge from the Blood River heritage site. Simultaneously, on the other side, President Zuma enters the bridge with his impressive entourage, including Zulu king Goodwill Zwelithini and Minister of Arts and Culture, Nathi Mthethwa. The two groups meet in the middle for the symbolic cutting of the ribbon.

Afterwards, celebrations take place on the Ncome side of the river. However, only a few Afrikaners attend, the majority opting to carry on with their usual traditions at the Blood River side.[4]

'Reconciliation is a process, and not an event,' says Zuma.[5]

* * *

A year later, celebrations on the two sides of the river continue to be separate and the bridge has yet to open. Since the inauguration, representatives of the Ncome and Blood River heritage sites have had several meetings, but so far they have failed to reach an agreement regarding how the bridge should be managed.[6]

And so there it lies, Reconciliation Bridge—its gates closed and its locks secured, in one last effort to keep the armies of past and future from crossing.

NOTES

1. RISE OF THE SUBURBAN FORTRESS

1. Rian Malan, *Resident Alien* (Jonathan Ball Publishers, Johannesburg & Cape Town, 2009), p. 250.
2. Ibid., p. 100.
3. United Nations Office on Drugs and Crime, *Global Study on Homicide* (Vienna, 2013), p. 124. Available at: https://www.unodc.org/documents/gsh/pdfs/2014_GLOBAL_HOMICIDE_BOOK_web.pdf
4. Alec Russell, *After Mandela: The Battle for the Soul of South Africa* (Windmill Books, London, 2010), p. 122.

16 DECEMBER 1838: THE BATTLE OF BLOOD RIVER

1. Hermann Giliomee, *New History of Africa*, 2012. Accessed at: http://newhistory.co.za/hermann-giliomee
2. Ibid.
3. Ibid.
4. Joseph Conrad, *Heart of Darkness* (Penguin Popular Classics Edition, London, 1994), p. 9.
5. Rian Malan, *My Traitor's Heart: Blood and Bad Dreams: A South African Exile Explores the Madness in His Country, His Tribe and Himself* (The Bodley Head, London, 1990), p. 13.
6. Ibid., p. 25.
7. Giliomee, *New History of Africa*, 2012.
8. Giliomee, *The Afrikaners: Biography of a People* (Hurst, London, 2010), pp. 144–49.

9. See Johannes Meintjes, *The Voortrekkers: The Story of the Great Trek and the Making of South Africa* (Cassell & Co., London, 1973).

16 DECEMBER 1866: THE RIVER TO REST

1. Line Gronstad, 'One Battle, Two Museums: the Ncome Bloedrivier Heritage Site,' *Msunduzi Journal* vol. 2 (Msunduzi/Voortrekker & Ncome Museums, Pietermaritzburg, 2010), p. 6.

4. THE NEW HOMELAND, ORANIA

1. Giliomee, *The Afrikaners*, pp. 560–61.
2. Chris McGreal, 'A people clutching at straws', *The Guardian*, (29 January 2000). Available at: https://www.theguardian.com/books/2000/jan/29/books.guardianreview3
3. See 'Van spookdorp tot droomdorp: Die verhaal van Orania': http://www.orania.co.za/wie-is-ons/geskiedenis/

16 DECEMBER 1881: THE RISE OF AFRIKANER NATIONALISM

1. Line Gronstad, 'One Battle, Two Museums. A study of cultural discourses and categorizations at Bloedrivier and the Ncome Heritage Sites in South Africa.' (2009), p. 6.
2. Giliomee, *The Afrikaners*, p. 396 & p. 432.

5. THE NEW TREK

1. Aislinn Laing, 'Farm work is South Africa's 'most dangerous occupation', *The Telegraph* (16 January 2015). Available at: http://www.telegraph.co.uk/news/worldnews/africaandindianocean/southafrica/11351055/Farm-work-is-South-Africas-most-dangerous-occupation.html
2. Johan Burger, 'Why it is more dangerous to be a farmer than a policeman in SA', Africa Check (6 November 2013). Available at: https://africacheck.org/2013/11/06/why-it-is-more-dangerous-to-be-a-farmer-than-a-policeman-in-south-africa/
3. Hassan Isilow, 'Over 1,000 white farmers murdered in SA since 1990',

Anadolu Agency (27 April 2016). Available at: http://aa.com.tr/en/world/over-1–000-white-farmers-murdered-in-sa-since-1990-/562158

4. Muchena Zigomo, 'S.Africa farmers sign Congo farmland deal', Reuters (20 October 2009). Available at: http://www.reuters.com/article/ozatp-safrica-congo-land-idAFJOE59J0I120091020

5. Reports available for download at http://hdr.undp.org/en/indicators/153706

6. SABC, 'Minimum wage may force N West farmers to shed jobs', (12 February 2013). Available at: http://www.sabc.co.za/news/a/467a78804e86d16299869bb7074a8d3f/Minimum-wage-may-force-N-West-farmers-to-shed-jobs

7. Thalia Holmes, 'New land reform Bill—dangerous or not?' *Mail & Guardian* (23 June 2014). Available at: http://mg.co.za/article/2014-06-23-new-land-expropriation-bill-dangerous-or-appropriate

8. Kate Wilkinson, Nechama Brodie, Sintha Chiumia & Julian Rademeyer, 'President Jacob Zuma's sixth State of the Nation address fact-checked,' Africa Check (14 February 2011). Available at: https://africacheck.org/reports/a-first-look-at-president-jacob-zumas-2014-state-of-the-nation-address

9. Holmes, 'New land reform Bill—dangerous or not?'.

6. GOOD WHITES, POOR WHITES

1. Annika Björnsdotter Teppo, *The Making of a Good White: A Historical Ethnography of the Rehabilitation of Poor Whites in a Suburb of Cape Town* (Gaudeamus University of Helsinki Press, Helsinki, 2004), p. 87.

2. Ibid., p. 117.

3. Ibid., p. 16.

4. Ibid., pp. 144–50.

5. Ibid., p. 152.

6. Ibid., p. 117.

7. Ibid., pp. 114–17.

8. Ibid., p. 139.

9. Documents of the Board of the Citizen's Housing League and the Social Welfare Committee (1938), in Björnsdotter Teppo, p. 146.

10. Björnsdotter Teppo, The Making of a Good White, p. 146.
11. Ibid.

7. CASTAWAYS OF THE RAINBOW NATION

1. Chris McGreal, 'A people clutching at straws', *The Guardian*, (29 January 2000). Available at:https://]www.theguardian.com/books/2000/jan/29/books.guardianreview3

8. VAGINA DENTATA

1. Carolyn Dempster, 'Rape—silent war on SA women,' BBC News (9 April 2002). Available at: http://news.bbc.co.uk/2/hi/africa/1909220.stm
2. Rachel Jewkes, Yandisa Sikweyiya, Robert Morrell, and Kristin Dunkle, *Understanding Men's Health and Use of Violence: Interface of Rape and HIV in South Africa*, South African Medical Research Council (Cape Town, 2009).
3. See http://rapecrisis.org.za/about-rape

9. SHOWER MAN

1. Alec Russell, After Mandela: The Battle for the Soul of South Africa (Windmill Books, London, 2010), p. 235.
2. Ibid., p. 246–47.
3. Ibid., p. 250.
4. Ibid., p. 252.
5. Ibid., p. 237.
6. Rian Malan, 'South Africa: a nation on the verge of collapse,' *Montreal Gazette*, (18 November 2006).
7. Victor Lindbom, 'Jas-mutor utreds på nytt,' *Dagens Nyheter*. (31 July 2011). Available at: http://www.dn.se/ekonomi/jas-mutor-utreds-pa-nytt
8. Sapa, 'Germans paid SA R300m for submarines, says report,' *Mail & Guardian* (5 August 2011). Available at: http://mg.co.za/article/2011-08-05-germans-paid-sa-r300m-for-submarines-says-report
9. Sapa, 'Seriti Commission costs you R80m,' Times LIVE (25 November

2014). Available at: http://www.timeslive.co.za/politics/2014/11/25/seriti-commission-costs-you-r80m

10. Jonas Cullberg, 'Nya protester mot Jas-utredning,' *Dagens ETC* (15 October 2014). Available at: http://www.etc.se/utrikes/nya-protester-mot-jas-utredning

16 DECEMBER 1938: 'N VOLK HELP HOMSELF

1. Giliomee, *The Afrikaners*, p. 432.
2. Ibid., pp. 441–45.
3. Ibid.
4. Ibid.
5. Ibid.
6. Ibid.
7. Ibid., p. 454.
8. Ibid., pp. 447–60.
9. Ibid., pp. 486–91.
10. Sheila Patterson, *The Last Trek: A Study of the Boer People and the Afrikaner Nation* (Routledge, London, 2013), p. 280.
11. Giliomee, *The Afrikaners*, pp. 475–76.
12. Ibid.
13. Ibid.
14. Ibid., p. 465.
15. Ibid., pp. 450–53.
16. Ibid., pp. 479–80.
17. Ibid.
18. Ibid., p. 482.
19. Ibid., p. 446.

10. BLOOD BROTHERS

1. Terry Bell with Dumisa Buhle Ntsebeza, *Unfinished Business: South Africa, Apartheid, and Truth* (Verso, London, 2003), p. 29.
2. Ivor Wilkins and Hans Strydom, *The Super-Afrikaners: Inside the Afrikaner Broederbond* (Jonathan Ball Publishers, Johannesburg & Cape Town, 2012), p. 343.

3. Ibid., pp. 1–2.
4. Ibid., p. 343.
5. Ibid., pp. 2–3.
6. Ibid., p. 345.

12. AN INCONVENIENT YOUTH

1. Sapa, 'Malema's supporters run riot', *Mail & Guardian* (30 August 2011). Available at: http://mg.co.za/article/2011–08–30-malemas-supporters-run-riot

2. Interview with Lucy Holborn, Research Manager at the South African Institute of Race Relations, 8 December 2011.

3. Fiona Forde, *An Inconvenient Youth Julius Malema and the 'New' ANC* (Portobello Books, 2011).

4. Ido Lekota, 'I am part of the ANC elite, Malema', *Sowetan* (1 December 2008). Available at: http://www.sowetanlive.co.za/sowetan/archive/2008/12/01/i-am-part-of-the-anc-elite-malema

5. '"Shoot the boer" song banned', News24 (26 March 2010), Available at: http://www.news24.com/SouthAfrica/News/Shoot-the-boer-song-banned-20100326

6. Deon de Lange, 'Malema: White people are criminals', IOL (8 May 2011). Available at: http://www.iol.co.za/news/politics/malema-white-people-are-criminals-1065708

13. SHOOT THE BOER

1. Interview with Ernst Roets, Deputy CEO of AfriForum, 1 December 2011.

2. Sapa, 'Malema stands to attention as he's sworn in,' News24 (21 May 2014). Available at: http://www.news24.com/elections/news/malema-stands-to-attention-as-hes-sworn-in-20140521

3. Amogelang Mbatha and Mike Cohen, 'South Africa Parliament Ejects Malema for Massacre Comments,' Bloomberg (20 June 2014). Available at: http://www.bloomberg.com/news/2014–06–20/south-africa-parlia-ment-ejects-malema-for-calling-anc-murderers.html

4. 'Julius Malema calls for full South Africa mining strike,' BBC News

(11 September 2012). Available at: http://www.bbc.co.uk/news/world-africa-19563096

14. GOOD FENCES MAKE GOOD NEIGHBOURS

1. Giliomee, *The Afrikaners*, p. 505
2. Ibid., pp. 503–4.
3. Ibid., pp. 511–13.
4. Ibid., pp. 482–500.
5. Ibid., pp. 484–519.
6. Ibid., pp. 515–32.

16 DECEMBER 1949: THREAT LEVEL: RED

1. Giliomee, *The Afrikaners*, pp. 488–99.
2. Ibid., p. 548.
3. Ibid., pp. 488–99; 548.

15. THE REVEREND

1. The South West Africa People's Organisation was founded in Windhoek in 1960 as a national liberation movement. Now a political party, SWAPO has governed the country since independence in 1990. The SWAPO Party of Namibia rejected the colonial moniker of 'South West Africa' and so no longer goes by its full name.
2. Giliomee, *The Afrikaners*, p. 606.

16 DECEMBER 1961: THE SECOND BATTLE FOR BLOOD RIVER BEGINS

1. Giliomee, *The Afrikaners*, p. 533.

16. TURNING A BLIND EYE

1. Giliomee, *The Afrikaners*, p. 600.
2. Ibid., p. 612.
3. Ibid., p. 604.
4. Ibid., pp. 612–23.

5. Malan, *Resident Alien* (Jonathan Ball Publishers, Johannesburg & Cape Town, 2009), p. 269.

6. Malan, *My Traitor's Heart: Blood and Bad Dreams: A South African Exile Explores the Madness in His Country, His Tribe and Himself* (The Bodley Head, London, 1990), pp. 272–73.

7. Ibid., pp. 222–24.

8. Ibid., pp. 221–22.

9. In 2014, Tim du Plessis left Media24, after 38 years, and joined kykNET.

10. Malan, *My Traitor's Heart*, p. 271.

18. THE BEGINNING OF THE END

1. As quoted by Max du Preez in his introduction to the 2012 edition of *The Super-Afrikaners: Inside the Afrikaner Broederbond* (Jonathan Ball Publishers, Johannesburg & Cape Town, 2012) by Ivor Wilkins and Hans Strydom, pp. xxviii-xxix.

16 DECEMBER 1988: TAINTED STORY, FADING GLORY

1. Interview with Tim du Plessis, Johannesburg, 4 May 2012.

2. Wilkins and Strydom, *The Super-Afrikaners: Inside the Afrikaner Broederbond* (Jonathan Ball Publishers, Johannesburg & Cape Town, 2012), pp. 12–13.

3. Giliomee, *The Afrikaners*, pp. 608–23.

4. Ibid., pp. 535–44.

5. Ibid., p. 611.

6. Ibid., pp. 656–64.

7. Ibid., p. 656.

8. Ibid., p. 664.

16 DECEMBER 1998: MUSEUM-JACKING

1. Paula Girshick, 'Ncome/Bloedrivier/Blood River: Nation-building and ethnic nationalism in post-apartheid South Africa,' *Msunduzi Journal* vol. 1 (Msunduzi/Voortrekker & Ncome Museums, Pietermaritzburg, 2008), pp. 45–49.

2. Line Gronstad, 'One Battle, Two Museums. A study of cultural discourses and categorizations at Bloedrivier and the Ncome Heritage Sites in South Africa.' (2009), p. 8.
3. Girshick, 'Ncome/Bloedrivier/Blood River,' p. 47.

20. THE BROTHERS OF SUNSHINE CORNER

1. Giliomee, *The Afrikaners*, p. 683.

21. AFFIRMATIVE ACTION

1. See the decision of the constitutional court, *South African Police Service v Solidarity obo Barnard*, pp. 6–7. Full report available for download at: http://www.saflii.org/za/cases/ZACC/2014/23.pdf
2. Press release of Solidarity trade union, *Solidarity takes Barnard case to Constitutional Court*, 2 November 2012.
3. Interview with Renate Barnard, 13 July 2016.
4. Sisonke Msimang, 'Affirmative Action in the New South Africa: The Politics of Representation, Law and Equity,' Isis International. Available at: http://www.isiswomen.org/index.php?option=com_content&view=article&id=644:affirmative-action-in-the-new-south-africa-the-politics-of-representation-law-and-equity8&catid=126&Itemid=452
5. Ibid.
6. Giliomee, *The Afrikaners*, p. 657.
7. Ibid., p. 701.
8. 'Race, law and poverty in the new South Africa,' *The Economist* (30 September 1999). Available at: http://www.economist.com/node/244570
9. Angela Quintal, 'Sacrifice winning for change, says Stofile', IOL (17 February 2005). Available at: http://www.iol.co.za/news/politics/sacrifice-winning-for-change-says-stofile-234203
10. Giliomee, *The Afrikaners*, p. 689.
11. Ibid., p. 702.
12. 'Race, law and poverty in the new South Africa,' *The Economist*.
13. Msimang, 'Affirmative Action in the New South Africa'.
14. 'S Africa Chinese "become black",' BBC News, (18 June 2008). Available at: http://news.bbc.co.uk/2/hi/africa/7461099.stm

22. THE BROEDERBOND: BETRAYED AND REBORN

1. Wilkins and Strydom, *The Super-Afrikaners: Inside the Afrikaner Broederbond* (Jonathan Ball Publishers, Johannesburg & Cape Town, 2012), p. 377.
2. Du Preez, Introduction to *The Super-Afrikaners*, pp. xviii-xix.
3. Wilkins and Strydom, *The Super-Afrikaners*, pp. 430–33.
4. Du Preez, Introduction to *The Super-Afrikaners*, p. xv.

16 DECEMBER 2006: A NAME-CALLING FIGHT

1. *Address of the President of South Africa, Thabo Mbeki, on the occasion of the ceremony to hand over to the nation, Isikhumbuto: Freedom Park, Salvokop, Tshwane, 16 December 2006.* Available at: http://www.gov.za/t-mbeki-reconciliation-day-isikhumbuto-freedom-park-handover
2. Sten Rylander, *Nelson Mandela—tolerans och ledarskap* (Historiska Media, Sweden, 2012), p. 256.
3. Sapa, 'Name change hearings slammed,' News24 (18 March 2010). Available at: http://www.news24.com/SouthAfrica/Politics/Name-change-hearings-slammed-20100318
4. Elwyn Jenkins, *Falling into Place: The Story of Modern South African Place Names* (David Philip Publishers, Cape Town, 2007), p. 155.
5. Ibid., pp. 155–56.
6. Ibid., p. 156.
7. Ibid., pp. 156–57.
8. Frans van der Merwe, 'With all the money they wasted, they could have built their own town,' Zoutnet (12 September 2008). Available at: http://www.zoutnet.co.za/articles/news/6715/2008–09–12/with-all-the-money-they-wasted-they-could-have-built-their-own-town
9. Sapa, 'Louis Trichardt name-change wrangle continues,' IOL (13 April 2007). Available at: http://www.iol.co.za/news/politics/louis-trichardt-name-change-wrangle-continues-1.322939#.VL96-VrVvzI
10. Linda van der Westhuizen, 'Thousands say "no" to Makhado,' *Limpopo Mirror* (14 November 2011). Available at: http://www.limpopomir-ror.co.za/articles/news/9891/2011-11-14/thousands-say-no-to-makhado

11. Sapa, 'Makhado's name reverts back to Louis Trichardt,' News24 (31 October 2014). Available at: http://www.news24.com/SouthAfrica/News/Makhados-name-reverts-back-to-Louis-Trichardt-20141031

12. Isaac Murwa-wa-Murwamuila, 'Louis Trichardt name change discussed again,' SABC News (14 November 2014). Available at: http://www.sabc.co.za/news/a/3a3a08004632d0b0bc97fc998462b36e/Louis-Trichardt-name-change-discussed-again-20141411

13. See the World Bank statistics on the distribution of income or consumption as an indicator of development. Available at: http://wdi.worldbank.org/table/2.9#

14. Paula Girshick, 'Ncome/Bloedrivier/Blood River: Nation-building and ethnic nationalism in post-apartheid South Africa,' *Msunduzi Journal* vol. 1 (Msunduzi/Voortrekker & Ncome Museums, Pietermaritzburg, 2008), p. 39.

16 DECEMBER 2008: AFRIKANER REVIVALISM

1. Gronstad, 'One Battle, Two Museums,' p. 10.

2. Chris McGreal, 'Gold mines shut as South Africa forced to ration power supply,' *The Guardian* (26 January 2008). Available at: https://www.theguardian.com/world/2008/jan/26/southafrica.international

25. THE BATTLE FOR HISTORY

1. In 2014, the book was published in English as *The History of South Africa: From the Distant Past to the Present Day* (Protea Boekhuis, Cape Town).

2. Nathi Olifant, 'ANC rewriting history—Buthelezi', *Sunday Tribune* (6 May 2012). Available at: http://www.iol.co.za/news/politics/anc-rewriting-history—buthelezi-1290035

3. Ibid.

26. THE *REAL* AFRICA

1. See Unicef's overview of HIV/Aids in eastern and southern Africa: http://www.unicef.org/esaro/5482_HIV_AIDS.html

16 DECEMBER 2011: A TALE OF TWO MUSEUMS

1. Line Gronstad, 'One Battle, Two Museums. A study of cultural discourses and categorizations at Bloedrivier and the Ncome Heritage Sites in South Africa.' (2009), p. 13.

29. A QUESTION OF SURVIVAL

1. Giliomee, *The Afrikaners*, p. 699.
2. Antjie Krog, *Country of My Skull*, London: Vintage, 1999, p. 238.
3. Giliomee, *The Rise and Possible Demise of Afrikaans as a Public Language*, PRAESA Occasional Papers No. 14 (PRAESA, University of Cape Town, 2003), p. 5. Available at: http://www.praesa.org.za/files/2012/07/Paper14.pdf
4. Giliomee, *The Afrikaners*, p. 474.
5. Interview with Tim du Plessis, Johannesburg, 4 May 2012.

AFTERWORD

1. *Address by President Zuma on the occasion of the unveiling of Ncome Phase 2 project during the National Day of Reconciliation, 16 December 2014.* Available at: http://www.thepresidency.gov.za/pebble.asp?relid=18670
2. Ibid.
3. Interview with Cecilia Kruger, 13 July 2016.
4. Ibid.
5. Address by President Zuma, 16 December 2014.
6. Interview with Cecilia Kruger.

SELECT BIBLIOGRAPHY

Books and Reports

Bell, Terry, with Dumisa Buhle Ntsebeza, *Unfinished Business: South Africa, Apartheid, and Truth* (Verso, London, 2003).

Björnsdotter Teppo, Annika, *The Making of a Good White: A Historical Ethnography of the Rehabilitation of Poor Whites in a Suburb of Cape Town* (Gaudeamus University of Helsinki Press, Helsinki, 2004).

Coetzee, J.M., *Waiting for the Barbarians* (Vintage Random House, London, 2004).

Conrad, Joseph, *Heart of Darkness* (Penguin Popular Classics Edition, London, 1994).

Forde, Fiona, *An Inconvenient Youth: Julius Malema and the 'New' ANC* (Portobello Books, London, 2011).

Giliomee, Hermann, *The Afrikaners: Biography of a People* (Hurst, London, 2010).

———, *New History of Africa*, 2012. Accessed at: http://newhistory.co.za/hermann-giliomee/

———, *The Rise and Possible Demise of Afrikaans as a Public Language*, PRAESA Occasional Papers No. 14 (PRAESA, University of Cape Town, 2003). Available for download at: http://www.praesa.org.za/files/2012/07/Paper14.pdf

Jenkins, Elwyn, *Falling Into Place: The Story of Modern South African Place Names* (David Philip Publishers, Cape Town, 2007).

Jewkes, Rachel, Yandisa Sikweyiya, Robert Morrell and Kristin Dunkle,

SELECT BIBLIOGRAPHY

Understanding Men's Health and Use of Violence: Interface of Rape and HIV in South Africa (South African Medical Research Council, Cape Town, 2009).

Krog, Antjie, *Country of My Skull* (Vintage, London, 1999).

Malan, Rian, *My Traitor's Heart: Blood and Bad Dreams: A South African Exile Explores the Madness in His Country, His Tribe and Himself* (The Bodley Head, London, 1990).

———, *Resident Alien* (Jonathan Ball Publishers, Johannesburg & Cape Town, 2009).

Mandela, Nelson, *Conversations with Myself* (Farrar, Straus & Giroux, New York, 2010).

Meintjes, Johannes, *The Voortrekkers: The Story of the Great Trek and the Making of South Africa* (Cassell & Co., London, 1973).

Patterson, Sheila, *The Last Trek: A Study of the Boer People and the Afrikaner Nation* (Routledge, London, 2013).

Russell, Alec, *After Mandela: The Battle for the Soul of South Africa* (Windmill Books, London, 2010).

Rylander, Sten, *Nelson Mandela—tolerans och ledarskap* (Historiska Media, Sweden, 2012).

United Nations Office on Drugs and Crime, *Global Study on Homicide* (Vienna, 2013). Available for download at: https://www.unodc.org/documents/gsh/pdfs/2014_GLOBAL_HOMICIDE_BOOK_web.pdf

Wilkins, Ivor and Hans Strydom, *The Super-Afrikaners: Inside the Afrikaner Broederbond* (Jonathan Ball Publishers, Johannesburg & Cape Town, 2012).

World Health Organization, *World Report on Violence and Health*, Chapter 6: Sexual Violence (Retrieved April 2015). Available at: http://www.who.int/violence_injury_prevention/violence/global_campaign/en/chap6.pdf

Articles

BBC News, 'South Africa's rape shock' (19 January 1999). Available at: http://news.bbc.co.uk/1/hi/world/africa/258446.stm

———, 'S Africa Chinese "become black"' (18 June 2008). Available at: http://news.bbc.co.uk/2/hi/africa/7461099.stm

————, 'Julius Malema calls for full South Africa mining strike' (11 September 2012). Available at: http://www.bbc.co.uk/news/world-africa-19563096

Burger, Johan, 'Why it is more dangerous to be a farmer than a policeman in SA,' Africa Check (6 November 2013). Available at: https://africa-check.org/2013/11/06/why-it-is-more-dangerous-to-be-a-farmer-than-a-policeman-in-south-africa

Cullberg, Jonas, 'Nya protester mot Jas-utredning,' Dagens ETC (15 October 2014). Available at: http://www.etc.se/utrikes/nya-protester-mot-jas-utredning

Daley, Suzanne, 'At Inauguration, Mbeki Calls for Rebirth of South Africa', *The New York Times* (17 June 1999). Available at: http://www.nytimes.com/1999/06/17/world/at-inauguration-mbeki-calls-for-rebirth-of-south-africa.html

De Lange, Deon, 'Malema: White people are criminals,' IOL (8 May 2011). Available at: http://www.iol.co.za/news/politics/malema-white-people-are-criminals-1065708

Dempster, Carolyn, 'Rape—silent war on SA women,' BBC News (9 April 2002). Available at: http://news.bbc.co.uk/2/hi/africa/1909220.stm

The Economist, 'Race, law and poverty in the new South Africa' (30 September 1999). Available at: http://www.economist.com/node/244570

Girshick, Paula, 'Ncome/Bloedrivier/Blood River: Nation-building and ethnic nationalism in post-apartheid South Africa,' *Msunduzi Journal: A journal of the Msunduzi/Voortrekker & Ncome Museums*, vol. 1 (Msunduzi/Voortrekker & Ncome Museums, Pietermaritzburg, 2008).

Gladdis, Keith, 'South African police reveal 34 miners died and 78 were wounded when armed officers opened fire on strikers,' *The Daily Mail* (16 August 2012). Available at: http://www.dailymail.co.uk/news/article-2189367/Marikana-strike-Police-gun-striking-South-African-miners-killing-30-leaving-scores-wounded.html

Gronstad, Line, 'One Battle, Two Museums: the Ncome Bloedrivier Heritage Site,' *Msunduzi Journal: A journal of the Msunduzi/Voortrekker & Ncome Museums*, vol. 2 (Msunduzi/Voortrekker & Ncome Museums, Pietermaritzburg, 2010).

Holmes, Thalia, 'New land reform Bill—dangerous or not?' *Mail & Guardian* (23 June 2014). Available at: http://mg.co.za/article/2014-06-23-new-land-expropriation-bill-dangerous-or-appropriate

Isilow, Hassan, 'Over 1,000 white farmers murdered in SA since 1990,' Anadolu Agency (27 April 2016). Available at: http://aa.com.tr/en/world/over-1–000-white-farmers-murdered-in-sa-since-1990-/562158

Laing, Aislinn, 'Farm work is South Africa's "most dangerous occupation",' *The Telegraph* (16 January 2015). Available at: http://www.telegraph.co.uk/news/worldnews/africaandindianocean/southafrica/11351055/Farm-work-is-South-Africas-most-dangerous-occupation.html

Lekota, Ido, 'I am part of the ANC elite, Malema,' *Sowetan* (1 December 2008). Available at: http://www.sowetanlive.co.za/sowetan/archive/2008/12/01/i-am-part-of-the-anc-elite-malema

Lindbom, Victor, 'Jas-mutor utreds på nytt,' *Dagens Nyheter* (31 July 2011). Available at: http://www.dn.se/ekonomi/jas-mutor-utreds-pa-nytt

Malan, Rian, 'South Africa: a nation on the verge of collapse,' *Montreal Gazette* (18 November 2006).

Mbatha, Amogelang and Mike Cohen, 'South Africa Parliament Ejects Malema for Massacre Comments,' Bloomberg (20 June 2014). Available at: http://www.bloomberg.com/news/2014–06–20/south-africa-parliament-ejects-malema-for-calling-anc-murderers.html

Mbeki, Thabo, *Address of the President of South Africa, Thabo Mbeki, on the occasion of the ceremony to hand over to the nation*, Isikhumbuto: Freedom Park, Salvokop, Tshwane, *16 December 2006*. Available at: http://www.gov.za/t-mbeki-reconciliation-day-isikhumbuto-freedom-park-handover

McGreal, Chris, 'A people clutching at straws,' *The Guardian* (29 January 2000). Available at: https://www.theguardian.com/books/2000/jan/29/books.guardianreview3

——, 'Gold mines shut as South Africa forced to ration power supply,' *The Guardian* (26 January 2008). Available at: https://www.theguardian.com/world/2008/jan/26/southafrica.international

Msimang, Sisonke, 'Affirmative Action in the New South Africa: The Politics of Representation, Law and Equity,' Isis International. Available at: http://www.isiswomen.org/index.php?option=com_content&view=a

rticle&id=644:affirmative-action-in-the-new-south-africa-the-politics-of-representation-law-and-equity8&catid=126&Itemid=452

Murwa-wa-Murwamuila, Isaac, 'Louis Trichardt name change discussed again,' SABC News (14 November 2014). Available at: http://www.sabc.co.za/news/a/3a3a08004632d0b0bc97fc998462b36e/Louis-Trichardt-name-change-discussed-again-20141411

News24, '"Shoot the boer" song banned' (26 March 2010). Available at: http://www.news24.com/SouthAfrica/News/Shoot-the-boer-song-banned-20100326

Olifant, Nathi, 'ANC rewriting history—Buthelezi,' *Sunday Tribune* (6 May 2012). Available at: http://www.iol.co.za/news/politics/anc-rewriting-history—buthelezi-1290035

Quintal, Angela, 'Sacrifice winning for change, says Stofile,' IOL (17 February 2005). Available at: http://www.iol.co.za/news/politics/sacrifice-winning-for-change-says-stofile-234203

Smith, David, 'Marikana mine shootings revive bitter days of Soweto and Sharpeville,' *The Guardian* (7 September 2012). Available at: http://www.theguardian.com/world/2012/sep/07/marikana-mine-shootings-revive-soweto

South African Broadcasting Corporation (SABC), 'Minimum wage may force N West farmers to shed jobs,' (12 February 2013). Available at: http://www.sabc.co.za/news/a/467a78804e86d16299869bb7074a8d3f/Minimum-wage-may-force-N-West-farmers-to-shed-jobs

South African Press Association (Sapa), 'Louis Trichardt name-change wrangle continues,' IOL (13 April 2007). Available at: http://www.iol.co.za/news/politics/louis-trichardt-name-change-wrangle-contin-ues-1.322939#.VL96-VrVvzI

——, 'Name change hearings slammed,' News24 (18 March 2010). Available at: http://www.news24.com/SouthAfrica/Politics/Name-change-hearings-slammed-20100318

——, 'Germans paid SA R300m for submarines, says report,' *Mail & Guardian* (5 August 2011). Available at: http://mg.co.za/article/2011–08–05-germans-paid-sa-r300m-for-submarines-says-report

——, 'Malema backers run amok,' IOL (30 August 2011). Available at: http://www.iol.co.za/news/politics/malema-backers-run-amok-1127660

——, 'Malema's supporters run riot,' *Mail & Guardian* (30 August 2011). Available at: http://mg.co.za/article/2011–08–30-malemas-supporters-run-riot

——, 'Malema stands to attention as he's sworn in,' News24 (21 May 2014). Available at: http://www.news24.com/elections/news/malema-stands-to-attention-as-hes-sworn-in-20140521

——, 'Makhado's name reverts back to Louis Trichardt,' News24 (31 October 2014). Available at: http://www.news24.com/SouthAfrica/News/Makhados-name-reverts-back-to-Louis-Trichardt-20141031

——, 'Seriti Commission costs you R80m,' Times LIVE (25 November 2014). Available at: http://www.timeslive.co.za/politics/2014/11/25/seriti-commission-costs-you-r80m

Van der Merwe, Frans, 'With all the money they wasted, they could have built their own town,' Zoutnet (12 September 2008). Available at: http://www.zoutnet.co.za/articles/news/6715/2008–09–12/with-all-the-money-they-wasted-they-could-have-built-their-own-town

Van der Westhuizen, Linda, 'Thousands say "no" to Makhado,' *Limpopo Mirror* (14 November 2011). Available at: http://www.limpopomirror.co.za/articles/news/9891/2011–11–14/thousands-say-no-to-makhado

Wilkinson, Kate, Nechama Brodie, Sintha Chiumia and Julian Rademeyer, 'President Jacob Zuma's sixth State of the Nation address fact-checked,' Africa Check (14 February 2011). Available at: https://africacheck.org/reports/a-first-look-at-president-jacob-zumas-2014-state-of-the-nation-address

Zigomo, Muchena, 'S.Africa farmers sign Congo farmland deal,' Reuters (20 October 2009). Available at: http://www.reuters.com/article/ozatp-safrica-congo-land-idAFJOE59J0I120091020

Zuma, Jacob, *Address by President Zuma on the occasion of the unveiling of Ncome Phase 2 project during the National Day of Reconciliation, 16 December 2014*. Available at: http://www.thepresidency.gov.za/pebble.asp?relid=18670